BEN FRANKLIN

FOR BEGINNERS®

BEN FRANKLIN

FOR BEGINNERS®

BY
TIM E. OGLINE

FOR BEGINNERS®

For Beginners LLC
155 Main Street, Suite 211
Danbury, CT 06810 USA
www.forbeginnersbooks.com

A For Beginners® Documentary Comic Book

Copyright © 2013

Cataloging-in-Publication information is available from the Library of Congress.

ISBN # 978-1-934389-48-5 Trade

Manufactured in the United States of America

For Beginners® and Beginners Documentary Comic Books®
are published by For Beginners LLC.

First Edition

10 9 8 7 6 5 4 3 2 1

Scan the QR code
with your QR reader
enabled smartphone to visit
For Beginners® online.

BEN FRANKLIN FOR BEGINNERS

TABLE OF CONTENTS

Bust of Benjamin Franklin
Jean-Antoine Houdon, 1779

If you would not be forgotten,

as soon as you're dead and rotten,

either write things worth reading,

or do things worth the writing.

– BENJAMIN FRANKLIN, 1706-1790

Benjamin Franklin would accomplish a great deal in his 84 years... and certainly a whole lot worth writing about. In fact, according to the Library of Congress, there are at least 3,463 books currently in their collection (at this writing) that are catalogued with the keywords of "Benjamin Franklin." These include books written by, about, or make mention of... and that's just in English.

The beginning of a journey for a boy who would boldly swagger off to discover a new world would hold much in the way of adventure for a young man. The events that were to follow would become the stuff of legend.

Benjamin Franklin wore many hats during his long and illustrious life. He excelled at — and even defined — a number of professions, including: printer, writer, postmaster, scientist, inventor, public citizen, politician, and diplomat. (And speaking of hats, he made the beaver fur hat a fashion statement that Paris would never forget.)

He discovered practical uses for electricity. He was America's first great satirist. He founded the University of Pennsylvania. He invented bifocals. He was a legendary ladies' man. He was a cornerstone in the foundation of the United States of America. He made the case for war. And he also made peace.

The words and deeds of Benjamin Franklin, his folksy wisdom and his sage advice, still speak to us. They have become a core part of the American experience. One man who would ask himself "What good shall I do today?" with each morning, found a way to do good and defined moments and historic events that we're still talking about almost 300 years later.

I have been the more particular in this description of my journey that you may compare such unlikely beginnings with the figure I have since made there.
— Franklin to His Son

From an inscription on the pedestal of this forward looking statue depicting a young Ben Franklin at the beginning of his journey. The statue is located at 33rd Street, in front of Weightman Hall at the University of Pennsylvania in Philadelphia.

Youthful Franklin
sculpture by R. Tait McKenzie, 1914

PART ONE

BENJAMIN
and
BEGINNINGS

Benjamin Franklin was born on January 6, 1706 (or January 17, 1706 as it would later become) in Boston. He was the fifteenth of seventeen children growing up in the crowded Milk Street home of Josiah and Abiah Franklin.

The Franklin family hung their many hats in this house on Milk Street in Boston.

Josiah Franklin had wanted young Ben to become a minister since he was his tenth son and, hence, his "tithe" (defined as "a tenth part of something paid as a voluntary contribution or tax to the church") to the Lord (which Benjamin Franklin would one day recall with his tongue firmly in cheek). Josiah had determined that Ben would ultimately attend Harvard for his studies. Ben was sent to Boston Latin School for preparatory school. But there was just something about that

A new calendar system was introduced in 1582 by Pope Gregory XIII as a means to replace the Julian calendar. The new Gregorian calendar eliminated the leap year (years with February 29) from years that were divisible by 100, except for years divisible by 400 (therefore the years 1800 and 1900 would not be leap years, but the year 2000 would be).

The United Kingdom and her colonies adopted the Gregorian calendar in 1752, so ten days were removed from that year in the process of moving from the former Julian calendar system.

boy that did not seem well suited for the clergy, so Josiah eventually pulled young Ben from Boston Latin.

Josiah began to prepare the boy to be his apprentice and teach him the skills of candle and soap making. The strong-willed Ben was not particularly enthusiastic about this line of work and agitated for another profession. Josiah knew that Ben could run away as he had a "strong inclination for the sea" (as he had phrased it years later in his famous autobiography). The family was still reeling from Josiah Jr. being recently lost at sea. This caused Josiah to relent and assist his son in finding a discipline to which Ben was better predisposed.

Josiah took young Ben on a tour of trades. Ben observed cutlers, mechanics, bricklayers, and joiners, among others. Finally, Ben was apprenticed at age 12 to his older brother James in the printing trade.

James Franklin had returned from London in 1717 where he presumably worked as a journeyman printer. He brought back a press as well as collections of movable type and printing blocks and set to business with the backing of his father. The relationship between Ben and his older brother was not smooth. Benjamin was bright and headstrong and often clashed with his older brother and master. He considered him a bully and a harsh taskmaster. Many of the disputes were often presided over by their father in order to come to an accommodation between the belligerent brothers.

A breaking point occurred when James Franklin stirred up trouble with the newspaper that they produced, *The New England Courant*.

Many trades with highly refined skill sets required a route to reach the level of competency and mastery of a craft. Typically, a master craftsman would take on an apprentice. The apprentice usually would work for a period of 7 years in the service of their master as they learned their trade. An apprentice's compensation was generally their trade training as well as room and board.

After the apprentice has completed their service, they are then released from their service and graduate to the status of journeyman. A journeyman was free to seek work where he chose and would receive wages for his labor. The journeyman could also ultimately go on to set up his own shop and become a master himself.

The nature in which the paper challenged local authority caused the Boston government to issue an edict that barred James Franklin from publishing *The New England Courant*. The two brothers decided that Ben would publish *The New England Courant*. However, Ben needed to be freed of his indenture as an apprentice in order for him to officially become the paper's publisher. This was done, but Ben was made to sign a new, secret indenture to his brother that committed him to his original term of indenture until he was twenty-one years old.

Ben expected that with his official release from indenture that James would not try to enforce a secret agreement. At seventeen, Ben decided to skip town... but only after his brother had warned other Boston printers not to hire Ben should he come looking for work.

Ben's inclination for the sea took him to the docks, and he conducted his departure from Beantown by boat. Franklin's fast-talking friend, John Collins had convinced the captain of a New York-bound sloop that Ben was on the run after getting a naughty girl in the family way and needed to get out of town (quietly).

NEW YORK, NEW YORK...

Here I come!

Boston was nicknamed "Beantown" due to the fact that baked beans were a hometown favorite and widely available. The abundance of molasses in Boston was an integral ingredient in Boston Baked Beans.

Boston was home of the largest seaport in America and the free flow of molasses occurred as part of the triangle trade which was defined as hard goods from Europe were shipped to and traded for slaves from Africa and on to the West Indies where the slaves were sold and sugar cane was bought and shipped to Boston to be fermented into rum. From Boston, Newfoundland Salt Cod and corn would be shipped back to Britain.

★ A BRAND NEW START OF IT ★

During the journey to New York, the sloop's progress was hindered by weak winds and the sailing trip was slowed. Ben soon found himself running out of his provisions. He began to hungrily eye the cod being pulled from the seas by his fellow travelers. As Ben was a vegetarian, he found the situation increasingly bothersome and found that his feelings of hunger were stronger than his sense of conviction.

Vegetarianism was one of Franklin's earliest self-improvement schemes. He had embraced the doctrine of vegetarianism while in the charge of his brother James. It was only in part a moral conviction to not eat of the flesh. His primary reason for not eating meat was that it was a really way to save money. A diet made up mainly of fruits and vegetables was far cheaper than the carnivorous kind. Since Ben had asked his brother to let him be responsible directly for his own meals, Ben could pocket the difference and buy books.

Ben noted some of his fellow travelers preparing a dinner from the ocean's bounty. He observed that the content of the fish's stomachs included a number of smaller fish. This was a revelatory moment and gave Ben the moral right to partake of the flesh: "If you eat one another, I don't see why we mayn't eat you."

If you eat one another....

I don't see why we mayn't **EAT YOU.**

Three days and 300 miles after putting Boston behind him, Franklin found himself in New York looking for work. He had difficulty finding employment, prospective or otherwise. Finally, William Bradford (1663-1752), a printer formerly of Philadelphia, told him to proceed there and seek out his son Andrew Bradford (1686-1742) for a solid job prospect.

★ PHILADELPHIA FLUNG ★

Philadelphia, which would become the world-renowned birthplace of American Independence and the cheese steak, became Ben's ultimate destination. Franklin's autobiography famously recounts his arrival in the City of Brotherly Love on October 6, 1723. He writes about the sight he made as a seventeen-year-old runaway walking down Philadelphia's Market Street with two large puffy rolls under each arm while somehow managing to eat the third. He also writes that he must have made a comical sight as he strolled by his future wife, Deborah Read, standing in the doorway of the rooming house of John Read where he would soon take up boarding.

> Then I walked up the street, gazing about till near the market-house I met a boy with bread. I had made many a meal on bread, and, inquiring where he got it, I went immediately to the baker's he directed me to, in Second Street, and ask'd for bisket, intending such as we had in Boston; but they, it seems, were not made in Philadelphia. Then I asked for a three-penny loaf, and was told they had none such. So not considering or knowing the difference of money, and the greater cheapness nor the names of his bread, I made him give me three-penny worth of any sort. He gave me, accordingly, three great puffy rolls. I was surpriz'd at the quantity, but took it, and, having no room in my pockets, walk'd off with a roll under each arm, and eating the other.

Philadelphia, founded in 1682 by William Penn (1644-1718), was the capital of Pennsylvania (until 1799) and the United States (until 1800). Philly's nickname of "The City of Brotherly Love" is the literal translation of the Greek words that comprise its name.

Thus I went up Market Street as far as Fourth Street passing by the door of Mr. Read, my future wife's father; when she, standing at the door, saw me, and thought I made, as I certainly did, a most AWKWARD RIDICULOUS APPEARANCE.

I turned and went down Chestnut Street and part of Walnut Street, eating my roll all the way, and, corning round, found myself again at Market Street wharf, near the boat I came in, to which I went for a draught of the river water; and, being filled with one of my rolls, gave the other two to a woman and her child that came down the river in the boat with us, and were waiting to go farther.

Franklin's follies upon coming to Philadelphia didn't end there. He wandered into a crowd, entered a Quaker meeting house, and sat among them. In short order, the road-weary Ben promptly fell asleep during the service.

Franklin did find work for a printer named Samuel Keimer (1689-1742) after being referred to him by Andrew Bradford. Ben didn't think much of Keimer's operation or the quality of his work, so he kept an eye out for other opportunities should they arise.

Young Franklin did come to the attention of Pennsylvania Governor Sir William Keith (1669-1749). This occurred because a concerned family friend of Franklin's wanted to convince the young man to return home. Keith took a liking to the industrious and ambitious young Franklin upon seeking him out at Keimer's. As he wanted to have a good printer in Philadelphia, Keith offered to help the lad set up shop and see to it that government business came Franklin's way.

Sir William Keith's place in posterity — for better or worse — has been permanently defined by the recollections of Benjamin Franklin in his autobiography.

At first, Keith provided Ben with a letter of endorsement and sent him back to Boston to get money from his father to purchase the essentials of the craft. Josiah Franklin denied his son the backing unless he could prove that he could save much of the necessary money by the age of twenty-one. His father then would only then lend him the balance to allow him to pursue this enterprise.

Josiah's decision didn't stop Ben, and Governor Keith took it upon himself to bankroll the operation. The governor promised to send letters of credit for passage and expenses. Ben would set sail for London in November 1724 to buy the presses, fonts, and other equipment needed for the printing profession.

Meanwhile, Franklin had begun courting Deborah Read, daughter of his landlord. He had also begun to discuss getting married. Deborah's mother wasn't entirely agreeable to this proposed union of her fifteen-year-old daughter and this eighteen-year-old. She thought that it may be best that any marriage be delayed until Ben's return from London.

★ LONDON TIMES ★

Upon Franklin's arrival in the London in December, he learned that there was no letter of credit forthcoming from his presumed patron. He also learned but that the well-meaning and impulsive Sir William Keith had no credit. Thus, without the money to pay for a return Atlantic trip, Benjamin Franklin, eighteen years old, was stranded in the Old Smoke.

As Franklin would one day write under the name Richard Saunders, "Diligence is the mother of good luck." Ben made the best of his

London had become known as "the Old Smoke" due to the number of wood and coal fires throughout the crowded city. The smoke spewing from home cooking and heating fires was trapped by the famous London fog rolling in off the Thames. It created thick, heavy smog that blanketed the metropolis.

circumstances. Thomas Denham, a Quaker merchant and a man who had traveled with Franklin on the *London Hope* across the Atlantic, recommended that Franklin seek out work at the prestigious Palmer's printing house.

Ben quickly was hired and became quite popular with his fellow pressmen at Palmer's. His colleagues valued him for his skills and his work ethic but perhaps more so as a practitioner of the art of frugality. Ben Franklin — who became known as the "Water American" due to the fact that he did not drink alcohol during working hours — made it a point to pinch his pennies and, thus, typically had ready coins in his pockets to lend for beer.

Interestingly enough, the "Water American" seemed to make quite a splash during his time across the Atlantic. He made it a daily task to swim in the Thames. He even gave an exhibition for his friends where he performed a series of strokes that would amaze and awe the onlookers. This "ornamental" swimming became a storied event and had Londoners seeking him out as a swim instructor.

Ben Franklin was inducted into the International Swimming Hall of Fame in 1968 for his contributions to aquatics including his "ornamental" swimming as well as his invention of swim fins in 1717.

Ben took to the cosmopolitan lifestyle and fast living of old London Town. He went to the theater, met with men of letters, loitered at cafés, and was making a name for himself among his fellow Londoners. Some of Franklin's friendships were of a less than noble nature. Franklin had later lamented in life of what he characterized as "intrigues with low women" during his days of London living. Benjamin Franklin would ultimately gain the reputation as a notorious womanizer. A number of biographers have, however, done some investigating to right the record and clean up Ben's image for posterity. The question of Franklin's flirtations and what is fact and what is fiction is somewhat inconclusive.

With all of Ben's bustling in far-away London, his letters home to Deborah amounted to just one. Meanwhile, because Ben's affections seemed to be engaged elsewhere, Deborah met and married a potter named John Rogers.

Thomas Denham, Franklin's shipmate from the *London Hope*, convinced Ben to return with him to Philadelphia. The Quaker merchant offered to pay for Ben's return passage as well as an annual stipend for his work as a clerk at Denham's general store. They had also discussed an arrangement that would ultimately sell the store to Ben in the future.

★ BACK TO PHILADELPHIA ★

Ben returned to Philadelphia in July 1726 and went to work straight away for Thomas Denham. Their plans made in far-off London didn't prove to bear fruit in the short run. Denham took ill within a few months and died. This unfortunate development left Ben without the means to take ownership of the store and to continue operations.

Franklin reluctantly went back to work for Keimer as manager in 1727. But when Ben eventually learned that Keimer had intended to let him go once he had trained his subordinates, he decided to finally make his move. He would pursue a partnership in the establishment of a printing business with a fellow Keimer employee, Hugh Meredith, in June 1728. The path that Franklin would pursue from this point forward would prove to bear considerable fruit for many years to follow.

Ben was also in negotiations to establish another partnership. He was courting the daughter of a fellow boarder of his rooming house (and client of his printing business). In the discussions of the prospects of marriage with the Godfrey family, Ben was insisting on a dowry (presumably to aid him in paying off his debts). The romance was ended as was as their friendship (which also resulted in the loss of a considerable printing job for Thomas Godfrey).

Ben's past love, Deborah (Read) Rogers came back into his life in due course. Ben and Deborah began living together (that would become a common-law union) at 139 Market Street in September 1730. Deborah's lawful husband, John Rogers, had reportedly run off to Barbados in 1728 to escape his creditors. Because it was unclear where Rogers was, there would have been some difficulties in enjoining a marriage in the event that he ever returned.

Two was company, but a third came to make a crowd in short order. Franklin presented Deborah with a baby boy from another mother.

Deborah Read Rogers Franklin

Things didn't get much better between Deborah and her stepson, William Franklin. Deborah's relationship with the lad could be characterized as one of grudging acceptance and was at times hostile. In fact, she at one time reportedly referred to William (who would one day become Royal Governor of New Jersey) as "the greatest villain upon the earth."

The Franklin home began to buzz and bustle even more when Deborah's mother joined the household in June 1731. Deborah and Ben did have a son of their own on September 20, 1732, Francis Folger Franklin. (He was a delight to his proud father, but tragically died from smallpox in November 1736). Ben's nephew, James Franklin, also joined the family after the untimely death of his father and Ben's brother James in 1737. The Franklin family would be further fortified with a daughter, Sarah, in 1743.

★ FRANKLIN FORWARD ★

Ben's journey from boy to man took lots of twists and turns: from Boston to New York to Philadelphia to London and back again to Philadelphia. From bold lad to runaway to self-made man and from rags to riches, the path of Benjamin Franklin would become the template for the American success story.

Franklin would make eight transatlantic journeys in his lifetime. He would return to London in 1757 under much better circumstances acting as agent for a number of American colonies as well as scientific celebrity. He would depart in 1762 and return in 1764 for an eleven year stay. Ben would also travel to Paris and remain there as an American Ambassador from 1776 to 1785. In all, Ben Franklin would spend some twenty-seven years overseas.

BENJAMIN AND BEGINNINGS:

A CHRONOLOGY

1657	Josiah Franklin (father) born in Ecton, Northamptonshire, England
1667	Abiah Franklin (mother) born in Nantucket, Massachusetts
1683	Josiah Franklin emigrates to Boston, Massachusetts
1689	Josiah Franklin and Abiah Folger marry
1706	Benjamin Franklin born in Boston, Massachusetts
1718	Begins apprenticeship to James Franklin (brother)
1723	Runs away from Boston, Massachusetts
	Arrives in Philadelphia, Pennsylvania
	Enters the employ of Samuel Keimer
1724	Sails to London, England
1726	Returns to Philadelphia, Pennsylvania
1727	Returns to the employ of Samuel Keimer
1728	Enters partnership with Hugh Meredith to establish printing business
1730	Benjamin Franklin and Deborah Read Rogers Franklin enter a common law marriage
1731	William Franklin (son) born
1732	Francis Folger Franklin (son) born
1736	Francis Folger Franklin (son) dies
1737	James Franklin (brother) dies
	James Franklin, Jr. (nephew) joins the Franklin household
1743	Sarah Franklin (daughter) born

This heroic bronze sculpture of young Benjamin Franklin at the printing press is located at the northwest corner of Broad Street and John F. Kennedy Boulevard across from City Hall in Philadelphia.

Benjamin Franklin, Craftsman
Joe Brown, 1981

PART TWO

PEN
and
PRESS

Benjamin Franklin's passion for printing sparked during his introduction to the trade as apprentice to his brother James from 1718 to 1723. It was dedication to this craft and the desire for the opportunity to excel within it — as well as to obtain his personal liberty — that drove him from Boston to seek his fortune elsewhere.

Even though Ben would officially retire from the trade, a wealthy man in 1748 at the age of forty-two, he would continue to say he was a printer — despite his achievements in other lines of work — until the end of his days.

At the age of just twenty-two, Franklin had even written this epitaph for his future self:

> The Body of
> B. Franklin
> Printer;
> Like the Cover of an old Book,
> Its Contents torn out,
> And stript of its Lettering and Gilding,
> Lies here, Food for Worms.
> But the Work shall not be wholly lost:
> For it will, as he believed, appear once more,
> In a new & more perfect Edition,
> Corrected and Amended
> By the Author.

> He was born on January 6, 1706.
> Died 17...

Benjamin Franklin may have certainly considered himself a printer first and foremost, but he was also an extremely gifted writer as well as a man who had a lot to say. Certainly, the trade of printing gave him the tools to do it.

It's been said that there are nine Muses — goddesses who inspire expression and creativity, ranging from poetry and music, to drama and dance, to arts and literature. But Franklin's Muse was likely not Calliope, Clio, Euterpe, or any of those nine we know. It was a Muse not of the nine: Necessity.

As a self-made man and as a doer, Franklin was predisposed to practicality. An idea would capture his imagination and he would set to it. He would let Necessity guide his way in discovering new ways to turn his thoughts and dreams into reality. The multi-faceted mind of Benjamin Franklin would work its way from the basic idea to an elegant solution. Franklin would employ this thought process in endeavors that were to entertain or enlighten with the printed page as well as those intended to improve the world around him with bigger and better ideas.

★ BEN'S BLACKBEARD BALLAD ★

For someone whose writing would one day catalyze change and influence generations around the world, the genesis of Benjamin Franklin's literary career was of a more modest nature. The 13-year-old Benjamin was encouraged to test his knack for rhyme by his older brother James. James thought Ben's verse clever and printed two of his poems as broadsheets, which Ben took to the streets and sold.

As Ben would later recall in *The Autobiography of Benjamin Franklin*, the poems included "The Lighthouse Tragedy" and "the other was a sailor's song, on the taking of Teach (or Blackbeard) the pirate":

Come all you jolly sailors,

You all so stout and brave;

Come hearken and I'll tell you

What happened on the wave.

Oh! 'Tis of that bloody Blackbeard
I'm going for to tell;
And as how by gallant Maynard
He soon was sent to hell.
With a down, down, down, derry down.

Franklin's father advised the boy against selling his verse in public places like some street urchin. Ben would concede that he was grateful for being shamed out of the practice as he had "escaped being a poet, most probably a very bad one."

The infamous Blackbeard is said to have woven lengths of smoldering hemp into his beard to give him a more devilish appearance.

★ LOOKING AT THE SPECTATOR ★

Ben Franklin would begin to seriously sharpen his skills as a writer in his Boston boyhood as a way of enhancing his powers of persuasion and to strengthen his ability for argumentation. The young Ben would often practice debating with his like-minded friend, John Collins, and learned that his capacity to convince was lacking.

Courtesy of LuEsther T. Mertz Library, the New York Botanical Garden

Franklin found inspiration in *The Spectator*, a London daily newspaper in which he would read the essays of Joseph Addison and Richard Steele. Ben would work to recreate the theme of some of their essays and refashion them in his own writing. This practice would help the future Franklin build a compelling case with the written word whether it be in effectively making his point, promoting a useful idea, or crafting a cunning hoax.

★ B . F R A N K L I N , P R I N T E R ★

Franklin's journey from runaway to self-made man gave him an appreciation for honest work and an affinity as tradesman. As a status-seeking young printer, he founded a social networking club called the Junto (otherwise known as the Leather Apron Club) in 1727. This gave him the opportunity to network with other young and ambitious up-and-comers.

One of Franklin's fellow Junto members was a fellow employee of Samuel Keimer, Hugh Meredith. Franklin and Meredith had often discussed a partnership. They ultimately left Keimer's employ to establish their own printing firm in 1728 with backing from Meredith's father.

The partners' early printing jobs were forms, pamphlets, and other small-scale pieces (which were at times exchanged for bartered goods). They also added to their revenue stream by selling letters and envelopes as well as books among other items from their printing shop on 139 Market Street in Philadelphia.

The pair found a way to secure a piece of the printing business for Pennsylvania that had so eluded and tantalized the younger Ben. The promise of a continuous stream of government business was a powerful motivator. It was just this carrot dangled by Pennsylvania Lieutenant-Governor Sir William Keith that took him to English shores just two years prior.

Andrew Bradford's printing firm had just published an address by the Governor to the General Assembly "in a coarse blundering manner" (as Franklin would describe it). Franklin and Meredith printed their own version ("elegantly and correctly") of the address in March 1729. They distributed copies to all members of the Assembly, demonstrating exceptional typographic design and composition as well as masterful presswork to demonstrate their distinction from their competitor. Franklin and Meredith soon secured all of the Province of Pennsylvania's official printing business on January 30, 1730. They also landed other contracts to provide official government printing for other colonies, including Delaware, Maryland, and New Jersey.

Franklin practiced the art of industry quite visibly in an effort to build a reputation as a hard worker to his fellow merchants and customers. He engaged in the conspicuous act of arriving early and leaving late from the printing shop of Franklin and Meredith to make just such an impression. He would also push heavy carts of rolls of paper through the streets to help reinforce this perception.

That Franklin fellow is QUITE *the Busy-Bee.*

BUSY-BODY, *the way I hear it.*

While Ben held to the principles of hard work and enterprise, his partner was not so diligent. Hugh Meredith was a little too fond of drink and not so predisposed to printing as it turned out. Ben bought out his partner's share of the business with the help of some friends on July 14, 1730. This gave Meredith the opportunity to move on to the pastoral splendor of North Carolina and to the life of a planter.

Benjamin Franklin's printing company would go on to great success for the twenty years that he would head the enterprise. The company would gain distinction for the superior craftsmanship and quality and would print government documents and currencies, legal forms, broadsides, newspapers, almanacs, pamphlets, and flyers. Franklin would also produce the first novel printed in America, *Pamela* by Samuel Richardson.

One of Franklin's showcase printing projects, CATO MAJOR.

Franklin ultimately chose to officially retire from the printing trade in 1748. He had entered into a partnership with his foreman, David Hall, who would continue to run the business. Ben remained an investment partner in the business until 1766.

Franklin had investment relationships with other printers in a number of colonies as well. In 1731, Franklin initiated the practice by patronizing his former journeyman, Thomas Whitmarsh (a compositor that Franklin had befriended in London). Ben set him up with a press in South Carolina in exchange for one-third of the profits over a six-year period. This became a business model that arguably establishes Benjamin Franklin as the father of printing franchising in America.

★ AND IN THE NEWS ★

When Ben Franklin and Hugh Meredith first decided to launch their own printing business, they had decided to start a newspaper as the core of their enterprise. Franklin sought to use his own experience working with his brother James, in publishing *The New England Courant*, the third newspaper to appear in Boston, in 1721. They thought it could compete with Andrew

The New England Courant was to be the third newspaper to appear in Boston in 1721. The *Courant* began publishing in 1721 and was created by James Franklin after losing the contract to print it to a competitor. This experience was clearly instructive for Ben Franklin, who would take a similar course in his own future printing business.

Bradford's *American Weekly Mercury* and believed that Philadelphia could be a two newspaper town.

Samuel Keimer, however, learned of the young men's plans through one of their fellow Junto members. He rushed his own paper to press, launching *The Universal Instructor in all Arts and Sciences: and Pennsylvania Gazette* on December 24, 1728. Franklin and Meredith were thwarted in their plan, as a third Philadelphia newspaper would face steep challenges in the battle for market share.

Andrew Bradford (who had first referred Ben to Samuel Keimer) launched THE AMERICAN WEEKLY MERCURY *in 1719, Pennsylvania's first newspaper.*

Franklin responded by engaging in a letter-writing campaign under the pseudonym of The Busy-Body to Bradford's *American Weekly Mercury* in order to cast ridicule and damage the reputation (thus weakening the condition) of Keimer's *Universal Instructor in all Arts and Sciences: and Pennsylvania Gazette*. This effort was designed to uneven the playing field between the two competing papers.

This operation was a practice Ben had a talent for and in which he had some considerable skill. Previously, the need for entertaining and lively content to increase circulation inspired a sixteen-year-old Benjamin Franklin to secretly write a series of fourteen letters to his brother's paper, *The New England Courant*. Ben used the name of Silence Dogood, a middle-aged widow and unrelenting nag and nitpicker. The letters rapidly drew an attentive following and increased the paper's readership (which annoyed James Franklin upon learning of the younger Franklin's ruse).

The combination of Franklin's snide scheme to erode the standing of the Gazette and Keimer's bad business practices drove Keimer out of business (and off to Barbados to escape his creditors). Franklin and Meredith purchased the failing paper (for a pittance) from their former employer. They then renamed it as *The Pennsylvania Gazette*. The pair published their first edition on September 25, 1729.

Ben did have some experience running a newspaper. During his apprenticeship to his brother James, he took the reins and published *The New England Courant* while James did some time in jail. James had openly mocked authority as well as criticized the clergy in the pages of the *Courant*, which put him on the wrong side of the law in the eyes of the town elders.

James' relations with the powers-that-be didn't improve much over time, and they soon barred him from printing the *Courant*. James and Ben hatched a plan whereby the paper would continue to be published under the name of B. Franklin until the prohibition on James and his editorship of *The New England Courant* had passed. However, when Ben handed back the reins of the operation to his brother, James expressed little gratitude for keeping the paper afloat. He also had lingering resentments about Ben's Silence Dogood campaign.

As with the Silence Dogood and The Busy-Body letters, Franklin wrote a number of articles for his own paper under assumed identities. Pen names like these were widely used and not particularly unusual in their usage. Readers had a similar indifference to the practice of publishing stories that were fanciful and outright fictitious among the factual in the pages of the news.

Franklin would learn that there were some times that messages needed to be delivered in a different package (for instance, to avoid resistance from the upper class against a modest tradesman) and that by disassociating ideas from his person and ego, the message may get a fairer and more open-minded hearing.

THE SATURDAY EVENING POST
An Illustrated Weekly Magazine
Founded A° D° 1728 by Benj. Franklin

Although *The Pennsylvania Gazette* ceased publication in 1800, the *Saturday Evening Post* has claimed the mantle of the Franklin legacy some 21 years later when it first went to print as a four-page newspaper and has asserted itself to be directly descended from *The Pennsylvania Gazette* today.

The Alumni Association of the University of Pennsylvania publishes an alumni magazine called *The Pennsylvania Gazette*, which began as *The Olde Penn* in November 1902.

One enduring essay from the pages of *The Pennsylvania Gazette* was Franklin's famed "Apology for Printers," published on May 31, 1731. Ben had a stock response to various criticisms regarding certain items that he brought to print. He offered up the "Apology" to explain why he had printed material that might have been counter to prevailing public tastes and opinions. He wrote:

> Being frequently censured and condemned by different Persons for printing Things which they say ought not to be printed, I have sometimes thought it might be necessary to make a standing Apology for my self, and publish it once a Year, to be read upon all Occasions of that Nature.

The "Apology" set a standard that good journalism tries to follow to this day, "Printers are educated in the Belief, that when Men differ in Opinion, both Sides ought equally to have the Advantage of being heard by the Public; and that when Truth and Error have fair Play, the former is always an overmatch for the latter: Hence they cheerfully serve all contending Writers that pay them well, without regarding on which side they are of the Question in Dispute."

Also in the pages of *The Pennsylvania Gazette*, Franklin created and published the very first American political cartoon on May 9, 1754. The "Join or Die" image accompanied an essay that illustrated the importance of the colonies uniting

JOIN, or DIE.

Courtesy of the Library of Congress

together for their mutual defense during the French and Indian War.

Ben also published the short-lived *Philadelphische Zeitung* beginning in 1732, America's first German-language newspaper.

★ MAKING MONEY ★

Benjamin Franklin was a big proponent of a paper currency, and he steered frequent discussions toward the topic in the Junto. He also had written and published a pamphlet in 1729 called *A Modest Inquiry into the Nature and Necessity of a Paper Currency*, which made the case for paper money. Franklin championed the system of having a paper currency that was backed by land holdings (as there was a fixed supply) and not tied to

A MODEST
ENQUIRY
INTO THE
Nature and *Necessity*
OF A
PAPER-CURRENCY.

Utilis Nummus habet ; *patriæ, charitæ, propinquis*
Quantum elargiri deceat. ———— *Pref.*

PHILADELPHIA:
Printed and Sold at the New PRINTING-
OFFICE, near the Market. 1729.

gold or silver (the supply of which was based on overseas trade and the availability of precious metals).

The good will engendered with the Pennsylvania General Assembly helped steer the contracts for the official printing of paper money to Franklin in 1731. Franklin would also obtain the printing contract to produce paper currency for Delaware in 1729. By 1736, Ben had picked up the printing of New Jersey money. He would also gain the official printing business for New Jersey in 1740.

A number of notes printed by Benjamin Franklin and partner David Hall as well by the succeeding firm of Hall and Sellers.

Benjamin Franklin made his inaugural appearance on the obverse (front) United States one hundred dollar bill in 1914. The one hundred dollar bill is currently the largest denomination in circulation since 1969.

Alexander Hamilton is the only other non-President to be featured on U.S. paper currency

Although counterfeiting was a capital offense punishable by death, it was a big problem that needed to be addressed. The British had even sought to exploit the issue and made an effort to destabilize the colonial economy. They tried to do this by circulating counterfeit cash into the system by sending bundles of the bogus bucks back with travelers to the Colonies during the Revolutionary War. Franklin had developed various methods to foil counterfeiters in printing of paper currencies. These included complex leaf designs as well as a number of varying spellings of "Pennsylvania" on differing denominations of the Keystone State's currency.

Courtesy of the Library of Congress

★ POOR RICHARD, RICH BENJAMIN ★

Almanacs were a thriving business in the Colonies. These annual publications included seasonal forecasts, astronomical calendars, practical advice, and folksy wit that made them indispensable in the colonial American household. It's been said that there were usually two books in every home: the *Holy Bible* and the current almanac.

Franklin had been printing some of these annual collections for customers, including Philadelphia farmer John Jerman and fellow Junto member Thomas Godfrey. After Franklin's ungallant insistence on the receipt of a dowry and his subsequent refusal to marry a young lady who was a relation of the Godfreys, Thomas Godfrey took his almanac and his business to competitor Andrew Bradford in 1729. John Jerman also took his *American Almanac* to Bradford as well.

Ben Franklin would heartily agree with Plato's assertion that necessity was the mother of invention. Franklin decided to create his own publication to replace the almanac business that he had lost. Necessity brought *Poor Richard's Almanac* to being and the first edition was published December 28, 1732.

Franklin's almanac was designed to be "entertaining and useful" in its presentation of content. One of the most enduring legacies of *Poor Richard's* would doubtlessly be the maxims in the margins. Typically, a blank space might appear on the page in the composing area between bodies of text, so Franklin would turn a phrase of an entertaining or useful nature to plug the hole. As Franklin put it, "chiefly such as inculcated industry and frugality, as the means of procuring wealth, and thereby securing virtue."

Many of the phrases plugged in the empty spaces of a page were not entirely original, but derived from antiquated sayings and made contemporary. Some of the familiar adages still quoted to this day include:

God HELPS
them that help THEMSELVES.

LOST TIME *is*
NEVER FOUND *again.*

He that lives upon HOPE
will DIE FASTING.

Beware of L I T T L E *expences,*
a small L E A K *will* S I N K
a G R E A T   S H I P .

T H R E E *may keep a* S E C R E T ,
if T W O *of them are* D E A D .

E A R L Y *to bed and*
E A R L Y *to rise,*
makes a man H E A L T H Y ,
W E A L T H Y *and* W I S E .

At its height, *Poor Richard's Almanac* sold more than 10,000 copies a year, making it one of one of the bestselling books in the American colonies. It also made Benjamin Franklin a very wealthy man. Franklin published the *Almanac* for twenty-five years, until the 1758 edition.

Ben collected the best of the adages culled from the twenty-five year run of *Poor Richard's* and published it as *Father Abraham's Speech* in 1758 (this was also later released as *The Way to Wealth*). The pithy proverbs were strung together in the form of a sermon delivered by Father Abraham on the virtues of frugality and industry.

Courtesy of Yankee Publishing Inc.

THE OLD FARMER'S ALMANAC — founded in 1792 by Robert B. Thomas and now published by Yankee Publishing — carries on the almanac tradition to this day with America's best known ongoing almanac.

Poor Richard — the *Almanac*'s friendly host and Franklin's alias — himself recounts the speech of Father Abraham, delighting in the entire address and ends, with Franklin's characteristic self-deprecation:

> Thus the old gentleman ended his harangue. The people heard it, and approved the doctrine, and immediately practiced the contrary, just as if it had been a common sermon; for the vendue opened, and they began to buy extravagantly, notwithstanding all his cautions, and their own fear of taxes.

The Way to Wealth has been continually in print, with more than 1,300 editions, since 1758. It has become one of the best-selling books of all time.

Almanacs were big business in the American colonies and POOR RICHARD'S ALMANAC was a best-seller for Benjamin Franklin, selling more than 10,000 annually.

★ MAGAZINE MISADVENTURE ★

Benjamin Franklin began one of America's first magazines, *The General Magazine and Historical Chronicle for all the British Plantations in America*, in 1741. The magazine wasn't much more successful than competitor Andrew Bradford's *America Magazine*, which only just barely preceded Franklin's and lasted just three issues. Franklin's decision to go into the magazine market went on for only six issues of the title before the *General* ceased publication as well.

★ PUBLIC PAMPHLETEER ★

In 1747, Franklin plied his pen to promote the public good. Ben's powers of persuasion went to work for the public defense when he authored and published an anonymous (but attributed to "A Tradesman of Philadelphia") pamphlet called *Plain Truth*. The pamphlet powerfully made the case for the establishment of a Pennsylvania militia. The militia would be responsible for providing a common defense against marauding French and Spanish privateers.

Quakers in the Pennsylvania Assembly were reluctant to fully fund an armed force; it went against their pacifistic tendencies. Franklin's anonymous pamphlet was successful in moving members of the Assembly to support the measure. Even more important, it caused the citizenry to contribute to the cause. Thus, the government and the people joined together to support the volunteer Pennsylvania militia for the protection of Pennsylvania and its people.

In another campaign of public spirited pamphleteering, Franklin introduced an innovative idea for the people of Philadelphia. Franklin's *Proposals Relating to the Education of Youth in Pennsylvania* of 1749 lamented that there wasn't a college of distinction among academic institutions in

Pennsylvania. Ben solicited the support of concerned citizenry and asked them to donate money to improve the education of youth. This led to the founding of the Academy of Pennsylvania in 1751, which later became known as the University of Pennsylvania in 1791.

Courtesy of the Library of Congress

Benjamin Franklin's very first pamphlet was more an exercise in youthful intellectual conceit than an effort of civic engagement. As a young man of nineteen in London, Franklin published his first tract, *A Dissertation on Liberty and Necessity, Pleasure and Pain.* The *Dissertation* was written as a rebuttal to a job that he had composed and typeset in the course of his employ at Palmer's Printing House (*The Nature of Religion Deliniated, 2nd Edition* by William Wollaston).

Benjamin Franklin wrote on the nature of God and free will with great fervor — and came to regret his exuberance and naïveté. After printing and distributing a few hundred copies of the *Dissertation*, Ben reconsidered his public pronouncements and he scrambled to reel them back in. In his embarrassment of the now-disowned *Dissertation*, he sought out and burned as many copies he could lay his hands on.

★ ELECTRIFYING THE WORLD ★

The year 1751 would transform Benjamin Franklin from an accomplished tinkerer into a worldwide celebrity in scientific and learned circles. Franklin was keenly interested in electrical phenomena and devoted a great deal of his early retirement to the study of it. He shared his observations on the subject in a series of letters to his friend Peter Collinson in London that discussed his experimentation in detail.

The letters were subsequently collected and published in one volume that won international acclaim. The eighty-six page *Experiments and Observations on Electricity, Made at Philadelphia in America*, edited by Dr. John Fothergill, was published in five English editions, three in French, one in Italian, and one in German .

★ BEN ON BEN ★

Benjamin Franklin worked on his autobiography off and on from 1771 to 1772 and 1784 to 1785. He returned to it yet again in 1788. *The Autobiography of Benjamin Franklin* began by using the literary convention of a long letter, addressed to his estranged son, William. This was meant to be instructive — the son, William Franklin, Governor of New Jersey, was a very proud man. Ben wanted his autobiography to show the path of his rise from humble beginnings as a runaway lad to the lofty heights he had accomplished through perseverance and hard work.

In 1777, during the Revolutionary War, a working manuscript of what would become one of the world's most praised and influential autobiographies was nearly lost. The British had taken the High Street home of the Franklins as a headquarters. The pages were tossed out, but were recovered by a Franklin friend who had happened to take notice of Ben's crumpled handwritten pages in the street.

The *Autobiography* is a classic of American literature. Even though it only covers some sixty percent of Franklin's life up to the age of fifty-one and ends with the arrival of Benjamin and son William in London on July 27, 1757, it is the great American success story. It's the memoir of the making of a self-made man.

The Autobiography of Benjamin Franklin was first published as *Mémoires de la vie privée de Benjamin Franklin*, in France in March 1791. The *Autobiography* was then translated back into English and published in London in 1793.

Mark Twain comically asserted that ruination afflicted the lives of boys everywhere upon their fathers reading *The Autobiography of Benjamin Franklin*.

His maxims were full of animosity toward boys. Nowadays a boy cannot follow out a single natural instinct without tumbling over some of those everlasting aphorisms and hearing from Franklin on the spot. If he buys two cents worth of peanuts, his father says, "Remember what Franklin has said, my son, — 'A groat a day's a penny a year;'" and the comfort is all gone out of those peanuts. If he wants to spin his top when he is done work, his father quotes, "Procrastination is the thief of time." If he does a virtuous action, he never gets anything for it, because "Virtue is its own reward." And that boy is hounded to death and robbed of his natural rest, because Franklin said once in one of his inspired flights of malignity:

Early to bed and early to rise
Make a man healthy and wealthy and wise.

As if it were any object to a boy to be healthy and wealthy and wise on such terms. The sorrow that that maxim has cost me through my parents' experimenting on me with it, tongue cannot tell. The legitimate result is my present state of general debility, indigence, and mental aberration. My parents used to have me up before nine o'clock in the morning, sometimes, when I was a boy. If they had let me take my natural rest, where would I have been now? Keeping store, no doubt, and respected by all.

PEN AND PRESS:

A CHRONOLOGY

1718	Becomes apprentice printer to James Franklin
1719	Prints and sells copies of his own poetry ("The Lighthouse Tragedy" and "The Taking of Teach the Pirate")
1721-23	Works on *The New England Courant*
1725	Publishes *A Dissertation on Liberty and Necessity, Pleasure and Pain*
1729	Publishes *The Nature and Necessity of a Paper Currency*
1728	Opens printing office at 139 Market Street, Philadelphia
1729	Begins publishing *The Pennsylvania Gazette* (founded by Samuel Keimer in 1723)
	Obtains contract to print Delaware currency
1730	Becomes official printer for Pennsylvania
1731	Begins printing franchise arrangement in South Carolina
	Founds the Library Company of Philadelphia
1732	Begins publishing *Poor Richard's Almanack*
1739	Moves printing office to 131 Market Street, Philadelphia
1740	Becomes official printer for New Jersey
1741	Begins publishing *The General Magazine and Historical Chronicle*
1747	Publishes *Plain Truth*
1748	Retires from printing
1749	Publishes *Proposals Relating to the Education of Youth in Pennsylvania*
1751	*Experiments and Observations of Electricity, Made at Philadelphia in America* published
1754	"Join, or Die," first American political cartoon, published in *The Pennsylvania Gazette*
1758	Publishes *The Way to Wealth*
1779	Proposes new translation of *The Holy Bible* by modernizing verses of "Job"
1791	*The Autobiography of Benjamin Franklin* first published in French
1793	*The Autobiography of Benjamin Franklin* translated into English

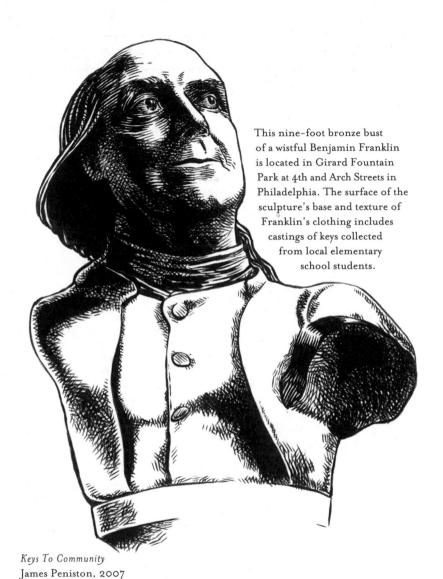

This nine-foot bronze bust of a wistful Benjamin Franklin is located in Girard Fountain Park at 4th and Arch Streets in Philadelphia. The surface of the sculpture's base and texture of Franklin's clothing includes castings of keys collected from local elementary school students.

Keys To Community
James Peniston, 2007

H U M O R I S T
and
H O A X S T E R

Ben Franklin stands as a prominent figure on the landscape of American humor and has been widely considered to be the first great American humorist. He formulated the friendly and folksy humor that would set the tone for the American style of the down-home wiseacre, chock full of common sense and without pretension. Succeeding generations of great American humorists and social satirists, including the likes of Mark Twain and Will Rogers, would have Benjamin Franklin to thank as their opening act.

Upon reading Franklin's recollections and reminisces, it's not entirely certain in some cases where the telling of a tale begins and where a tall tale may become part of the story.

Franklin would use his wit to carry out cunning hoaxes and pranks that would divert and bedevil friend and foe alike. Typically put to use for the purpose of social satire, Ben's humor often illustrated an absurdity with an absurdity. He would use it as a gentle prod to make a point sharply but without being hurtful.

WHO *shall I be today?*

Benjamin Franklin would adopt the role of many characters over his long and storied career of rascality. There are those he would write as or those he would write of as a means to use his ingenious wit to expose the harebrained and the featherbrained:

Alice Addertongue	Abigail Afterwit	Anthony Afterwit	Polly Baker
Benevolus	The Busy-Body	Martha Careful	Silence Dogood
Historicus	Sidi Mehemet Ibrahim	the King of Prussia	Harry Meanwell
Pacificus	Obidiah Plainman	Richard Saunders	Caelia Shortface
	Timothy Turnstone	Abigail Twitterfield	

Ben would typically adopt a persona or character when he wrote his clever allegories intended to challenge prevailing attitudes. This would be a lifelong vocation for Franklin. He started down this path at the age of sixteen and would carry on until he perpetrated his final hoax at the age of eighty-four — just two weeks before his death.

★   INTRODUCING SILENCE DOGOOD   ★

Benjamin Franklin's most celebrated hoax was directed squarely at his brother James, as well as at the people of Boston. Being just a boy of sixteen, Ben was barred from being a contributor to James' newspaper, *The New England Courant*. The paper carried mostly stories and pieces by the exclusive literary set that James Franklin and his friends admired and with whom they identified. Due to their sibling rivalry, the younger brother — and apprentice — was blocked from admittance to their exclusive group.

Ben created a character very far removed from the person that he was. He adopted the voice of a middle-aged preacher's widow by the name of Silence Dogood. He would write these correspondences and would slip them beneath his brother's printing shop door in the dark of night. Franklin would recall this long-run-ning prank with giddy elation years later in his autobiography:

I was excited to try my hand among them; but, being still a boy, and suspect-ing that my brother would object to print-ing anything of mine in his paper if he knew it to be mine, I contrived to disguise my hand, and, writing an anonymous paper, I put it in at night under the door of the print-ing-house. It was found in the morning, and communicated to his writing friends when they call'd in as usual. They read it, commented on it in my hearing, and I had the exquisite pleasure of finding it met with their approbation, and that, in their different guesses at the author, none were named but men of some character among us for learning and in-genuity. I suppose now that I was rather lucky in my judges, and that perhaps they were not really so very good ones as I then esteem'd them.

Ben's brother and his friends were quite taken with the caustic older woman and her catty commentary. They would publish these letters prominently in the *Courant*. They were so intrigued by the contributions of Silence Dogood that James Franklin made a public plea in the *Courant* for Mrs. Dogood to continue to submit additional letters to the paper.

This series of fourteen letters written to *The New England Courant* from April 2 to October 8, 1722 attacked hypocrisy and poked fun at the proper institutions of Boston. The tart-tongued writer would ridicule the young blockheads at Harvard or playfully write about the institution of marriage.

By way of introduction, Silence Dogood spoke of her character in her first early April letter to the *Courant*. She would further define her temperament in the closing of that first letter:

> Know then, That I am an Enemy to Vice, and a Friend to Virtue. I am one of an extensive Charity, and a great Forgiver of private Injuries: A hearty Lover of the Clergy and all good Men, and a mortal Enemy to arbitrary Government & unlimited Power. I am naturally very jealous for the Rights and Liberties of my Country; & the least appearance of an Incroachment on those invaluable Privileges, is apt to make my Blood boil exceedingly. I have likewise a natural Inclination to observe and reprove the Faults of others, at which I have an excellent Faculty. I speak this by Way of Warning to all such whose Offenses shall come under my Cognizance, for I never intend to wrap my Talent in a Napkin. To be brief; I am courteous and affable, good-humour'd (unless I am first provok'd,) and handsome, and sometimes witty.

Young Ben Franklin also took a mind to employ the Dogood device in the May 14, 1722 *Courant* in a letter that mocked the students of Harvard. The letter imparted his own smug superiority as well as revealed a certain degree of envy for those who had the opportunity to attend the institution that he could not:

> I reflected in my Mind on the extreme Folly of those Parents, who, blind to their Children's Dullness, and insensible of the Solidity of their Skulls, because they think their Purses can afford it, will needs send them to the Temple of Learning, where, for want of a suitable Genius, they learn little more than how to carry themselves handsomely, and enter a

Room genteelly, (which might as well be acquir'd at a Dancing-School,) and from whence they return, after Abundance of Trouble and Charge, as great Blockheads as ever, only more proud and self-conceited.

Ben enjoyed the laughter and praise James and his friends directed toward the mysterious Silence Dogood. The young men knew that many writers adopted pen names to disguise a writer's true identity — but little did they know that the author was none other than 16-year-old Benjamin Franklin.

Ben ultimately confessed that it was he who was the writer of the hugely popular letters. He subsequently took quite a scolding from his elder brother, as James was embarrassed in front of his friends that his little brother's ingenious stunt occurred entirely under his nose. Also, the generous praise heaped upon the previously unknown author of the Silence Dogood letters would make the younger Franklin vain and self-satisfied — and his older brother jealous of the boy's cleverness.

★ THE BUSY-BODY ★

On February 4, 1729, Franklin began a campaign in the pages of *The American Weekly Mercury* and created a gossip-monger who would publicly carp and quibble about his neighbors and the people of Philadelphia. He would say in this introductory letter that:

With more Concern have I continually observed the growing Vices and Follies of my Country-folk. And though Reformation is properly the concern of every Man; that is, Every one ought to mend One; yet 'tis too true in this Case, that what is every Body's Business is no Body's Business, and the Business is done accordingly. I, therefore, upon mature Deliberation, think fit to take no Body's Business wholly into my own Hands; and, out of Zeal for the Publick Good, design to erect my Self into a Kind of Censor Morum; proposing with your Allowance, to make Use of the *Weekly Mercury* as a Vehicle in which my Remonstrances shall be convey'd to the World.

The Busy-Body would continue to chatter in the pages of the *Mercury* for the coming months. There was a method to this *Mercury* madness.

Franklin would use the opportunity to take shots at Samuel Keimer's *Universal Instructor in Arts and Sciences: and Pennsylvania Gazette*. He did this in a number of the Busy-Body bulletins that also criticized the paper's credibility and its quality. The strategy was to steadily erode the readership of the *Gazette* while building up the *Mercury* with increased popularity and circulation. Over time, Keimer's paper was so weakened that he had to sell the paper to the partnership of Benjamin Franklin and Hugh Meredith.

Courtesy of the Library Company of Phil...

★ THE WITCHES OF JERSEY ★

On October 22, 1730, Benjamin Franklin took a poke at narrow-mindedness and puritanism of upright citizens in *The Pennsylvania Gazette*. He did this with an account of a fictional witch trial in nearby Mount Holly, New Jersey. Growing up in the shadow of the 1692 Salem Witch Trials, Franklin understood the unreasoning nature of the mob mentality that overwhelms levelheaded thinking.

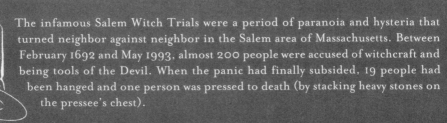

The infamous Salem Witch Trials were a period of paranoia and hysteria that turned neighbor against neighbor in the Salem area of Massachusetts. Between February 1692 and May 1993, almost 200 people were accused of witchcraft and being tools of the Devil. When the panic had finally subsided, 19 people had been hanged and one person was pressed to death (by stacking heavy stones on the pressee's chest).

But in this fictional witch trial, Franklin exposed the irrationality of the varying methods used to supposedly detect witchery. He did so by adding to his account a bit of common sense into the proceedings. This trial was conducted with the premise that those judging the "witches" would agree to submit to the same tests as the accused to display the contrast between the guilty and the innocent. Thus, the onlookers quite logically concluded that:

> The more thinking Part of the Spectators were of Opinion, that any Person so bound and plac'd in the Water (unless they were mere Skin and Bones) would swim till their Breath was gone, and their Lungs fill'd with Water. But it being the general Belief of the Populace, that the Womens Shifts, and the Garters with which they were bound help'd to support them; it is said they are to be tried again the next warm Weather, naked.

In the end, Franklin showed with his story that these occasions were no more than vulgar spectacles — which were the primary reasons that these trials were conducted in the first place.

★ ALMANAC ATTACK ★

In 1732, Ben created yet another alias known as Richard Saunders (a.k.a. Poor Richard). Saunders was to be a folksy persona who would be the voice of the almanac. He provided a personable and comical narrator — who was ever at the mercy of his badgering bride, Bridget — to introduce the *Almanac* each year. The name of Richard Saunders was actually derived from the name of the editor of British almanac, *Apollo Anglicanus* (or *The English Apollo*). The "Poor" portion of the name was borrowed from the *Poor Robin's Almanac*, published by brother James Franklin.

Andrew Bradford also published one of the most popular almanacs of the day, the *American Almanac*, by Titan Leeds (1699-1738). There were five other Philadelphia almanacs published at that time. This made for tough competition, so Franklin engineered a stunt in his inaugural edition of

Poor Richard's Almanac that predicted the time and date of Leeds' death in 1733. What better way to attract attention than to tweak your biggest rival? Leeds responded with scorn, publicly ridiculing Poor Richard and Benjamin Franklin. He assured everyone that he was still very much alive.

Franklin gleefully responded to the scorn of Titan Leeds. He asserted that there was no doubt that Titan Leeds was no longer among the living.

The person that was vilifying Richard Saunders would have had to been an impostor as Titan Leeds was too well bred and was too much a gentleman to ever attack him in such a manner. The publicity stunt attracted a great deal of attention and immediately set *Poor Richard's Almanac* apart from its competitors.

This flimflammery was actually inspired from the famous Bickerstaff Hoax. This was perpetrated by Jonathan Swift (1667-1745) under the name "Isaac Bickerstaff" in his 1708 *Bickerstaff's Almanac*. Swift dangled the same bait, predicting the coming death of competitor John Partridge of the *Merlinus Almanac* with similar results: Partridge was forced to try to convince others that he wasn't really dead.

★ GOOD FOR THE GOOSE ★

In the April 15, 1747 *General Advertiser*, Franklin took aim at the hypocrisy by which unmarried women were the subjects of scorn for having children outside of the sanctity of marriage. Men, it seems, that fathered these very children were largely spared these rebukes. The "Speech of Miss Polly Baker" was first published in the London paper and then reprinted over the coming months in *Gentleman's Magazine*, *Boston Weekly Post-Boy*, the *New York Gazette*, and the *Annapolis Maryland Gazette*.

> I have brought Five fine Children into the World, at the Risque of my Life: I have maintained them well by my own Industry, without burdening the Township, and could have done it better, if it had not been for the heavy Charges and Fines I have paid. Can it be a Crime (in the Nature of Things I mean) to add to the Number of the King's Subjects, in a new Country that really wants People? I own I should think it rather a Praise worthy, than a Punishable Action. I have debauched no other Woman's Husband, nor enticed any innocent Youth: These Things I never was charged with; nor has any one the least cause of Complaint against me, unless, perhaps the Minister, or the Justice, because I have had Children without being Married, by which they have miss'd a Wedding Fee. But, can even this be a Fault of mine?

In some versions of the retelling of Polly Baker's story, she so moves one of the magistrates with her clear logic that he marries her the next day after her acquittal. The story had a number of retellings in which it was said to be factual and had reportedly remained in circulation until 1917.

A chance encounter with Abbé Raynal (1713-1796), who had recounted the anecdote in his *Histoire Philosophique et politique des établissements et du commerce des Européens dans les deux Indes* [*Philosophical and political history and institutions of the European trade in the two Indies*], led Ben to confide to the French author that Polly's chronicle was pure concoction:

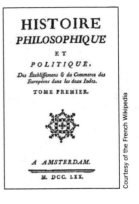

When I was a printer and editor of a newspaper we were sometimes slack of news, and to amuse our customers I used to fill up our vacant columns with anecdotes and fables and fancies of my own, and this tale of Polly Baker is one of my making.

★ THE OYSTER-EATING HORSE ★

Another example of Franklin's wry wit is on display in a tale that opens with Benjamin Franklin entering a Kingston, Rhode Island, tavern on a cold, rainy night. (This story presumably takes place during Ben's 1753 travels auditing postal routes during his days as Deputy Postmaster General of North America.) Franklin, upon surveying the huddled mass packed in around the welcoming fire, called out to the tavern boy and ordered a peck of oysters for his horse in the stable.

The boy looked back in confusion, but Ben urged him to hasten about the business. When the boy had exited the tavern, the curious crowd piled out behind him in order to see this amazing oyster-eating horse with their own eyes. A short time later, the boy returned and reported that the horse had refused the oysters.

Franklin, sitting smugly and snugly in front of the toasty fire, responded that he would take the oysters in that case and suggested that the boy give the horse some hay instead. The tavern patrons, now getting the joke, then joined Ben by the warmth of the glowing fire as he enjoyed his oysters after a hard day on the road.

This story may or may not be a tall tale, but Franklin certainly delighted in its telling.

★ FROM PRUSSIA WITH LOVE ★

As tempers flared and tensions rose between the colonies and England, Ben produced a prank in September 1773 that was supposedly the proclamation of Prussia's claims to England itself. "An Edict of the King of Prussia" put forth the notion that Great Britain was populated

The Kingdom of Prussia was founded in 1701 from the merging of Margraviate of Brandenburg and the Duchy of Prussia. Prussia would go on to dominate what was known as the German Empire until 1918 and the end of World War I when its lands were divided amongst other powers through the Treaty of Versailles. A reconstituted Free State of Prussia was later dissolved in 1947 after World War II by Allied Powers and the region has been largely absorbed by Germany and Poland.

by descendants of Prussians who had colonized the island nation. And thus, based on recently discovered ancient claims, England would be henceforth a protectorate of the Kingdom of Prussia:

> WHEREAS it is well known to all the World, that the first German Settlements made in the Island of Britain, were by Colonies of People, Subjects to our renowned Ducal Ancestors, and drawn from *their* Dominions, under the Conduct of Hengist, Horsa, Hella, Uffa, Cerdicus, Ida, and others; and that the said Colonies have flourished under the Protection of our august House, for Ages past, have never been *emancipated* therefrom, and yet have hitherto yielded little Profit to the same.

The King of Prussia from 1740 to 1786, Frederick II or "Frederick the Great" (1712-1786). Illustration based on the 1781 portrait by Anton Graff (1736–1813).

Franklin had crafted this bamboozlement as yet another of his masterful fictitious letters and dispatched it to *The Public Advertiser*, a London newspaper. The "Edict" scandalized the outraged Britons. The English were rightly angered that this "Edict" could make such demands on them with hefty taxes and burdensome restrictions on commerce (including such staples as iron and wool goods as well as on the trade of hattery). Of course, the entire exercise was meant to draw parallels between these outrageous false claims made by Prussia on Great Britain and the oppression by England that the American Colonies were protesting.

★ A FRIEND IN NEED ★

While in Paris in 1777, Ben was often presented with a request to send along a letter of recommendation to those who wanted to make the ocean voyage to America. And who better to give an account of one's character than the Great American himself: Benjamin Franklin? Ben, however, overwhelmed with these requests, created a form letter that really acted as a non-recommendation recommendation. Essentially, the letter said that I really don't know this person, but give them all the civility that you would a stranger and it's really up to you and your own judgment.

The Bearer of this who is going to America, presses me to give him a Letter of Recommendation, **THO' I KNOW NOTHING OF HIM,** *not even his name. This may be* **EXTRAORDINARY,** *but I assure you it is not uncommon here. Sometimes indeed one unknown Person brings me another equally unknown, to recommend him, and sometimes they* **RECOMMEND ONE ANOTHER!**

As to this gentleman, I may refer you to himself for his Character and Merits, with which he is certainly better acquainted than I can possibly be; I recommend him however to those civilities which every Stranger, of whom one knows no Harm, has a right to, and I request you will do him all the good Offices and show him all the Favour that on further Acquaintance you shall find him to deserve.

★ BOUT WITH THE GOUT ★

Benjamin Franklin composed a dialogue in October 1780 between himself and his most bedeviling enemy: the Gout. This exchange comically illustrates Franklin's attempt to justify and rationalize his behavior in the maintenance of his health to his own conscience.

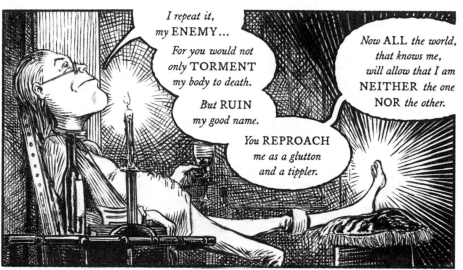

I repeat it, my ENEMY...

For you would not only TORMENT my body to death.

But RUIN my good name.

You REPROACH me as a glutton and a tippler.

Now ALL the world, that knows me, will allow that I am NEITHER the one NOR the other.

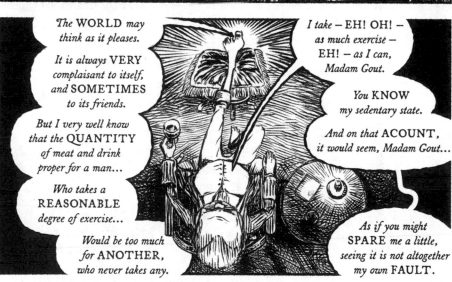

The WORLD may think as it pleases.

It is always VERY complaisant to itself, and SOMETIMES to its friends.

But I very well know that the QUANTITY of meat and drink proper for a man...

Who takes a REASONABLE degree of exercise...

Would be too much for ANOTHER, who never takes any.

I take — EH! OH! — as much exercise — EH! — as I can, Madam Gout.

You KNOW my sedentary state.

And on that ACCOUNT, it would seem, Madam Gout...

As if you might SPARE me a little, seeing it is not altogether my own FAULT.

Not a jot; your rhetoric and your politeness are thrown away; your apology avails nothing. If your situation in life is a sedentary one, your amusements, your recreations, at least, should be active. You ought to walk or ride; or, if the weather prevents that, play at billiards. But let us examine your course of life. While the mornings are long, and you have leisure to go abroad, what do you do? Wh_____ _____ _____ breakfast, by salutary-exercise, you amuse yourself with books, pamphlets, or newspap____ _____ _____ ___ding. Yet you eat an inordinate breakfast, four dishes of tea, with cream, a____ _____ _____ _____te____ which I fancy are not things the most easily digested. Immediately afterward ____ ____ ___ _____te_____ who apply to ___u on business. Thus the time passes till ____ _ _____ ___ __ _____ ___ _____ ____w to your _____tary condition. But what is your pr___ ____ af_____ _____ _____ ___ of ____ _____ _____uld be the chose_ __en of sense; yours is to be fixe__ __on to_____ ___ ____ ___ree hours! This is your perpetual recreation, which is the least eligible of ___ _ sedentary man, because ___stead_____ ___tion it requires helps to retard the circulation and obstruct internal secretions. Wrap_ ___ ___ulations of this un___d g___ _____ ___h a course of living but a body replete with stagnant humors, ready to fall a prey to all kinds of ___ ___ __is, if __ ___ G___ ___ ____ __ _____ __ purifying or dissipating them? If it was in some nook or alley in Paris, deprived of walks, that you played aw___ ___ ___ _____ _____ ___ ___Montmartre, or Sanoy, places where there are the finest gardens and walks, a pure air, beautiful women, and most agreeable and instructive _____ ___ __ ___nable game of chess. Fie, then, Mr. Franklin! But amidst my instructions, I had almost forgot to administer my wholesome corrections; so take that twinge— _____ ___

And on and on and on into the night, the two baited and debated...

59

★ SCALP TREATMENT ★

Franklin created another hoax for propaganda purposes in the pages of the *Supplement to the Boston Independent Chronicle*. This was a fake 1782 newspaper that Franklin had produced on his own press at Passy. The *Supplement* was created as a public relations ploy to gather support for the American Revolution in France and other European powers as well as from sympathizers in Britain.

The bogus broadsheet featured an extract of a letter from Captain Samuel Gerrish, a New England militia officer. The letter detailed the horrifying contents of packages intercepted en route to British General Frederick Haldimand, the Governor of the Province of Quebec. The captured containers reportedly included 1,062 scalps of Colonial soldiers, farmers, as well as women and children. These scalps had been purportedly obtained by Seneca Indians as an expression of their allegiance to the Crown.

★ TALKING TURKEY ★

Benjamin Franklin had serious misgivings about the Bald Eagle being exalted as America's national symbol. He expressed these views in a 1784 letter to his daughter, Sally (Mrs. Sarah Bache).

> For my own part I wish the Bald Eagle had not been chosen the Representative of our Country. He is a Bird of bad moral Character. He does not get his Living honestly. You may have seen him perched on some dead Tree near the River, where, too lazy to fish for himself, he watches the Labour of the Fishing Hawk; and when that diligent Bird has at length taken a Fish, and is bearing it

to his Nest for the Support of his Mate and young Ones, the Bald Eagle pursues him and takes it from him.

With all this Injustice, he is never in good Case but like those among Men who live by Sharping & Robbing he is generally poor and often very lousy. Besides he is a rank Coward: The little King Bird not bigger than a Sparrow attacks him boldly and drives him out of the District. He is therefore by no means a proper Emblem for the brave and honest Cincinnati of America who have driven all the King birds from our Country . . .

I am on this account not displeased that the Figure is not known as a Bald Eagle, but looks more like a Turkey. For the Truth the Turkey is in Comparison a much more respectable Bird, and withal a true original Native of America . . . He is besides, though a little vain & silly, a Bird of Courage, and would not hesitate to attack a Grenadier of the British Guards who should presume to invade his Farm Yard with a red Coat on.

★ SLAVERY SKIRMISH ★

Benjamin Franklin's hoaxes would extend until his final days. Franklin, writing as Historicus, sent a letter that was published in the March 23, 1790 edition of *The Federal Gazette*. It contained the supposed text of the "Address of Sidi Mehemet Ibrahim." The Address was said to be the words of Ibrahim, a member of the Algerian Divan (a high governmental body), spoken in 1687. In his Address Ibrahim made the argument for the continued capture and keeping of Christian slaves.

Franklin had created this counterfeit correspondence in response to a speech in *The Federal Gazette* by Congressman James Jackson of Georgia. Jackson had spoken before Congress, urging "against their meddling with the Affair of Slavery." Sidi Mehemet Ibrahim's Address made the case that because Muslims were so far superior to these pale-skinned barbarians, it was actually more humane for them to keep these captives in servitude. These Christian slaves would benefit immensely by the example of how a more advanced society acts as well as give them the opportunity to know the one true God in Allah.

If we cease our Cruises against the Christians, how shall we be furnished with the Commodities their Countries produce, and which are so necessary for us? If we forbear to make Slaves of their People, who in this hot Climate are to cultivate our Lands? Who are to perform the common Labours of our City, and in our Families? Must we not then be our own Slaves? And is there not more Compassion and more Favour due to us as Mussulmen, than to these Christian Dogs? We have now about 50,000 Slaves in and near Algiers. This Number, if not kept up by fresh Supplies, will soon diminish, and be gradually annihilated. If we then cease taking and plundering the Infidel Ships, and making Slaves of the Seamen and Passengers, our Lands will become of no Value for want of Cultivation; the Rents of Houses in the City will sink one half; and the Revenues of Government arising from its Share of Prizes be totally destroyed!

Of course, this satire was aimed squarely at supporters of slavery in the legislature and the people who voted for them. It was designed to show how morally empty arguments in support of the slave trade were and would continue to be. This final parting shot fired by Ben Franklin, President of the Pennsylvania Abolitionist Society, proved that his aim and wit were as precise as ever in confronting one of the greatest of moral failings of the first generation of Americans.

HUMORIST AND HOAXSTER:

A CHRONOLOGY

1722	Silence Dogood letters published in *The New England Courant*
1729	Busy-Body letters published in *The American Weekly Mercury*
1730	Publishes satire about a fictional Mount Holly, New Jersey witch trial in *The Pennsylvania Gazette*
1732	Predicts the death of rival almanac publisher Titan Leeds in *Poor Richard's Almanac*
1747	"Speech of Miss Polly Baker" published in the *General Advertiser*
1753	Pulls Oyster Eating Horse prank
1773	"An Edict of the King of Prussia" published in *The Public Advertiser*
1777	Distributes requested form letters of recommendation to aspiring acquaintances traveling to America
1780	Writes "Dialogue with the Gout"
1782	Publishes *Supplement to the Boston Independent Chronicle,* a faux newspaper for propaganda purposes in Paris
1784	Writes letter discussing merits of the Turkey as National Bird
1790	"Address of Sidi Mehemet Ibrahim" hoax published in *The Federal Gazette*

Benjamin Franklin Gargoyle
designed by
H.J. Hardenbergh, 1908

On the Palmer Physics Laboratory at Princeton University is this gargoyle depicting Benjamin Franklin with key and lightning bolt, commemorating Franklin's pioneering work in electricity.

PART FOUR

INNOVATOR
and
INVENTOR

The mind of Benjamin Franklin was restless, a veritable whirlwind of activity. Franklin had keen observational skills that allowed him to assess situations and make connections. He could thereby make intuitive leaps in imaginative and speculative thought that enabled practical problem solving. His powerful and creative intellect gave him the tools to figure out the task at hand and make it a reality.

This drive to create and improvise actually started quite early in his life. In fact, Ben invented swim fins at the age of eleven. It was part of the particular way that Ben Franklin's mind worked. He would question the conventional and wonder how to do things or make things better. Many of Franklin's breakthroughs were achieved through what we might call in the modern day "building a better mousetrap."

In many instances, he would appropriate and innovate. He would draw on his encyclopedic knowledge and on his experience in order to take an idea to make it relevant and useful. Innovation was behind his utilization of the odometer, his creation of bifocal glasses, and the introduction of much-improved street lighting to Philadelphia. This practice of "appropriate and innovate" could also be seen at work in his civic initiatives. It was also at work in the number of public improvements that he would propose and pursue for the people of Philadelphia and Pennsylvania.

Franklin's thought process went beyond engineering remarkable improvements in useful items and notions. It also exerted itself into areas unexpected and at times unprecedented. This is precisely the sort of thinking that gave us the lightning rod, the Franklin Stove, and the Glass Armonica. This is the thinking that found serviceable uses for electricity, that charted the Gulf Stream, and devised efficient practices and procedures for the colonial postal system.

Ben's brilliance wasn't just confined to a particular expertise or calling. Instead, it allowed him to be an ingenious generalist and Renaissance man. He was an adaptive thinker, capable of performing in varying specialties. His achievements are similar to the achievements of other famed polymaths, such as Leonardo da Vinci or Isaac Newton.

Franklin believed in sharing ideas and research with peers for the advancement of knowledge. He founded the American Philosophical Society in 1743 just for that purpose. Ben would also share the fruits of his labors for a number of inventions and innovations that are in use to this day. Franklin never patented or took a profit from his inventions: he considered them his gift to the people. Franklin wrote of this gift to his fellow man in his autobiography:

> As we enjoy great advantages from the inventions of others, we should be glad of an opportunity to serve others by any invention of ours; and this we should do freely and generously.

★ IN THE SWIM OF THINGS ★

Young Franklin was an avid swimmer and would take to the mill pond near his boyhood Boston home. In an effort to increase his speed — and likely inspired by the fins of the fish he swam with — he fashioned oval paddles to affix to his hands, as well as flippers fitted to his feet, to propel his watery travels.

The paddles for his hands actually slowed him down (although similar paddles are used today to strengthen swimmers by the increased resistance). But he did find that the flippers allowed him to swim faster. At age eleven, Benjamin Franklin invented the swim fin.

And although Ben Franklin would in the future become world-famous for something else in the history of kite flying, at an early age he first used a kite as a sail in order to move him across the pond.

★ FIRED UP ★

Ben was frustrated by the inefficiency of fireplaces in heating homes. Heat from a wood fire would mostly go through the chimney. At the same time, sparks from the fire were a considerable hazard in an era when most homes were constructed of wood. Thus, when faced with a practical problem, Franklin set his mind to the task of rethinking the fireplace. In 1742, he created a standalone cast iron fireplace that could be centrally located in a room and heat the space more evenly.

This kind of fireplace, which was also known as a circulating stove, was constructed in a manner that improved airflow and subsequently generated more heat and less smoke than a conventional fireplace. The first version of what Franklin called the Pennsylvania Fireplace had, however, a significant design flaw. Smoke came up out of the bottom of the fireplace and was vented up and out into the room. This flaw also dampened the flames in the firebox because it created a barrier to air being drawn in.

Even with the design flaw, the Pennsylvania Fireplace proved to be something that there was a demand for, since it was far better

Pennsylvania Fireplace

than the alternative of a fixed-wall fireplace. When Pennsylvania Governor George Thomas offered an exclusive patent to Franklin for the manufacture and sale of his creation, Ben declined and chose to make his invention public domain for the good of his fellow man. This

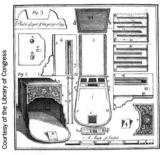

may have been one of the earliest examples of open-source culture for the purposes of making something available to all for further innovation. He provided the plans for production to his friend Robert Grace, who went on to manufacture them. He also published the pamphlet *An Account of the New Invented Pennsylvanian Fire-Places*. The pamphlet featured specifications for construction and use in order to make public the idea and help market his creation.

Plans for assembly of the Pennsylvania Fireplace from Franklin's pamphlet, AN ACCOUNT OF THE NEW INVENTED PENNSYLVANIAN FIRE-PLACES.

The stove was later improved upon by another Philadelphia notable, David Rittenhouse in 1772. Rittenhouse created an L-shaped flue that would vent the smoke out the back and up through a chimney. Rittenhouse's innovation led him to rename the Pennsylvania Fireplace as the Rittenhouse Fireplace. The once-flawed fireplace has undergone a number of improvements and has evolved into an even more efficient engine of heat with a closed firebox. The identification of the stove with Ben Franklin has persisted to modern times and led it to become eventually known as the Franklin Stove.

New and improved: the Franklin Stove.

★ TAMING THE ELECTRICAL FIRE ★

The colonial public showed a great deal of interest in demonstrations of practical natural philosophy in their exposure to and experience of science. At the time, a class of itinerant learned showmen performed public displays of electrical wonders that were more parlor tricks than pure science. But these "electricians," as they were called, raised public curiosity about the nature and action of "electrical fire."

Franklin's own fascination was captured in the science and spectacle of the new field of electricity through a series of lectures in 1744 conducted by Dr. Archibald Spencer (identified as Dr. Spence in Franklin's autobiography) in Philadelphia. Dr. Spencer performed public experiments during these lectures on natural curiosities, Newtonian mechanics, and electrical entertainments. The lectures were available in the form of paid subscriptions and Franklin acted as Spencer's agent in this enterprise. He published advertisements for the series in *The Pennsylvania Gazette* as well as collected subscription fees at the post office.

One of the most captivating exercises during these popular presentations occurred in the practice of electrifying persons, which was a real crowd pleaser. One such experiment centered on a boy suspended by silk strands in midair. The boy would gather a negative electric charge by rubbing his feet with a charged glass rod through electrostatic induction. As charge isn't generated, but transferred through a process Franklin would call "conservation of charge," an excess of electrons would build up in the suspended boy. At the same time, the glass rod would become positively charged due to the loss of electrons.

The origin of the word electricity stems from the Latin word "electricus," which was in turn based on the Greek word "elektron" (which meant "amber"). English physician William Gilbert coined the term in 1600 as a result of his observations of the attractive behavior of amber when rubbed. His experiments with amber demonstrated the characteristics of what would one day be known as static electricity.

Amber is fossilized tree resin and is widely used in jewelry.

As the boy was hanging in mid-air and not grounded, he was unaffected by any buildup of electrical charge. But a grounded person, who would extend their hand close to or touch the young man, would receive the boy's negative stored electrical charge and the discharge would create a shock to the grounded person. These and other similar demonstrations were exercises in electrical amusements, but piqued the curiosity of Benjamin Franklin and prompted him into a serious examination of these marvels.

Ben purchased Dr. Spencer's electrical equipment (presumably after Spencer had retired from performing and entered the ministry). He then began his own observations and experimentations with great enthusiasm in 1746. Some of Ben's principal tools for his analysis included, among other items, an electrostatic generator as well as Leyden jars.

Franklin had, additionally, begun some small experiments with static electricity prior to obtaining Spencer's apparatus. He made use of a gift of glass rod and silk cloth as well a German pamphlet on the topic in 1745 from Peter Collinson, a friend of the Library Company of Philadelphia and Fellow of the Royal Society.

Ben applied his observations from laboratory conditions to the outside world. He developed a theory that lightning may be less of a mythological thunderbolt hurled from the

The electrostatic generator consisted of a hand crank spinning wheel that would turn a pulley wheel above by way of a leather belt in a closed loop. The pulley wheel would rotate a glass sphere, which would create friction against a leather pad. The glass globe would then store a static electrical charge.

The earliest electrostatic generator was invented in the 1660s by Otto von Guericke (1602-1686) of Germany and was the first of class of friction machine as the charge was drawn through rubbing two objects together.

Electrostatic Generator

heavens and more of a force of nature. And this force of nature could be quantified through scientific examination as an expression of electricity.

Ever the great thinker and connector of concepts, Franklin devised a device that became known as the lightning rod (or in some quarters, Franklin rods) in 1750. The lightning rod — which Franklin said should be an eight- to ten-foot-long pointed metal rod — was intended to draw the "electric fire" from the sky above through the metal rod mounted to roofs, steeples, spires, and ship masts.

Of the two types of rod (protective and insulated) Franklin had created, the protective rod had a connective cable affixed to it that ran down to the ground. This conductive cable would be grounded to a fixed object or its end would be buried about ten feet into the ground. Upon a lightning strike, the massive electrical current would be conducted from the metal rod through the wire and safely dispersed into the ground below. It thereby bypassed the structure and those within.

Although it may seem entirely medieval to the modern mind, there was a tremendous amount of resistance to the lightning rod. People were reluctant to defy an "Act of God" by trying to deflect God's will in the form of a lightning bolt. It was seen as wicked and disrespectful of mere mortals to defy the plan of the Almighty if He was engaging in divine retribution by smiting a deserving sinner.

Church steeples were prone to lightning strikes as they were the tallest structures of any community. The steeples also housed a high concentration of conducting metal in the bells housed in the belfry, making it especially attractive to lightning. Conventional wisdom of the

Leyden jars were glass bottles with an outer and inner coating of metal foil as well as an electrode that extended from the bottle closure. This allowed for a charge to be drawn off the electrostatic generator and stored in the jar.

Dutchman Pieter van Musschenbroek (1692-1761) at the University of Leiden conceived of a device to act as capacitor to store charges which became known as the Leyden jar. Ben Franklin discovered that multiple jars wired in serial could store an even greater charge, which he would call a "battery."

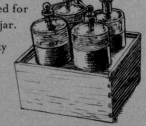

Leyden Jar Battery

time held that the ringing of church bells could dissuade judgment from on High coming down into their community. For some this was the preferred method to safeguard a community's steeples and people over the lightning rod. This, however, made bell-ringers much more vulnerable to bolts from the blue.

It was a church, in fact, where Franklin wanted to perform one of his most ambitious experiments. This exercise was intended to draw "electrical fire" from the storm clouds above through an insulated rod. This was central to Franklin's famous Sentry Box Experiment. The Sentry Box Experiment consisted of a lightning rod projecting from the peak of insulated booth (that was both sheltered and dry) perched atop a high building or steeple.

The occupant of the sentry box could draw off sparks from the charged rod without threat of harm as long as they weren't grounded (this is because the person would form part of the circuit and allow the electricity to flow through them). As an added precaution, Ben had recommended that the charge be drawn off with a wire insulated with a wax grip.

Franklin wanted to conduct the Sentry Box Experiment at Christ Church in Philadelphia. However, construction delays in completing the spire from which he wanted to perform this exercise forced him to consider another option. The alternative approach to Ben's original plan became one of the most legendary experiments in the annals of science: the Kite Experiment.

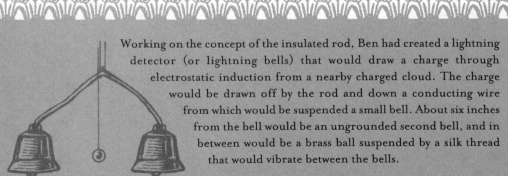

Working on the concept of the insulated rod, Ben had created a lightning detector (or lightning bells) that would draw a charge through electrostatic induction from a nearby charged cloud. The charge would be drawn off by the rod and down a conducting wire from which would be suspended a small bell. About six inches from the bell would be an ungrounded second bell, and in between would be a brass ball suspended by a silk thread that would vibrate between the bells.

Benjamin Franklin and his twenty-one-year-old son William took to a field in anticipation of a coming storm. They set about the business of drawing lightning from the angry sky above by sailing a kite to the height that the steeple was to have soared. The kite was fashioned out of two cedar cross bars, over which was stretched a silk handkerchief. A metal wire extended from the top end of the vertical cross bar, and from that the hempen twine would trail in its considerable length to a metal key.

Franklin piloted the kite while connected to the end of the twine by a nonconducting silk cord. He stood beneath a sheltered enclosure in order to stay out of the rain and remain dry. When the metal wire attached to the kite drew a charge by way of induction, it would travel through the rain-soaked twine and to the key. Franklin experienced the nature of the lightning as electrical phenomenon by holding his knuckle close to the key and drawing off sparks. From there, the Franklins gathered ample amounts of electrical charge with a number of Leyden jars.

SHOCKING!

Franklin's investigations into the nature of electrical phenomena through these experiments were recorded in a series of letters that he wrote to Peter Collinson (1694-1768). Collinson had read these letters before the Royal Society, but ultimately decided to collect them into one 86-page volume and published it as *Experiments and Observations on Electricity, Made at Philadelphia in America* in 1751.

Peter Collinson, illustration based on the 1783 engraving by T. Trotter.

The book set into motion an international sensation as English, French, German, and Belgian men of science began conducting the very experiments that Ben had discussed in his letters to Collinson. These independent experiments gave Franklin validation of his theories and observations. (There was one mishap, however, in the conducting of the Sentry Box Experiment. Professor Georg Wilhelm of St. Petersburg, Russia was electrocuted in 1753. He was grounded and not on an insulating stand.)

Some of Franklin's electrical undertakings were less high-minded and more hijinks. He electrified the champagne glasses of his guests at a dinner party to add an extra tingle to the bubbly. He also famously sought to electrocute a turkey for Christmas dinner in 1750, but was distracted during his preparations and ended up giving himself quite a shock. Ben also concocted other parlor tricks, such as an electrified portrait of King George III and dancing spiders for the amusement and delight of his visitors.

Benjamin Franklin's achievements brought him an elevated stature in the scientific community as well as international accolades and honors. In 1753, he was awarded the prestigious Copley medal from the Royal Society of London. Ben was also awarded a number of honorary degrees. He was inducted into numerous prestigious societies. Franklin's impact on the field of electricity has been long lasting. To this day the terms that Franklin applied to his observations, such as "positive," "negative," "charge," "condenser," "conductor," and "battery" are still used to discuss the forces he helped identify.

*Why, yes...
There is a
DOCTOR
in the house.*

Because of all the honors and degrees he received, Benjamin Franklin was addressed as Dr. Franklin by many. Ben may have been called "Doctor," but only in the academic sense and not of the medical variety — although he did conduct some work with "medical electricity." He would administer electroshock therapies by request to some suffering from palsies or numbness of limb. Franklin wasn't a serious practitioner and was somewhat skeptical of the practice.

★ MUSIC OF THE (HEMI)SPHERES ★

Playing musical glasses was a popular pastime in the parlors of London as well as at dinner parties throughout Europe. Musical glasses created a unique and distinctive sound, through harmonic vibrations created by stroking the brims of drinking glasses containing varying amounts of liquid. Ben was so charmed by the beautiful harmonies evoked from everyday drinking glasses that he set to constructing a device to achieve those same haunting melodies.

Franklin created this very device in 1761. The instrument used a horizontal rotating iron spindle that spun thirty-seven glass bowls of graduated sizes. These bowls were the medium on which the music was produced. This device allowed the operator to bring forth the song of musical glasses by stroking the spinning hemispheres with moistened fingers while controlling the spin by foot pedal. Each of the bowls was marked with bands of different colors to signify various notes.

The device was known as the Glass Armonica and became quite popular in Europe. Marie Antoinette reportedly took lessons on it. The infamous Franz Anton Mesmer would play the soothing sounds of the Glass Armonica in order to mesmerize his patients during their "treatments." (More about Mesmer on p. 84.) Wolfgang Amodeus Mozart, Ludwig van Beethoven, and Richard Strauss were among the many composers who were fascinated by the instrument and created music for it.

Franklin's instrument fell out of vogue once rumors began circulating — mostly coming from Germany — that those who used the device were increasingly being afflicted with a form of emotional distress. Some attributed these issues to possible lead poisoning contracted through the high-lead content in the glass, but that has never been substantiated.

Benjamin Franklin's Glass Armonica was the toast of Europe and made Franklin the Les Paul of his day.

★ A POSTAL MILESTONE ★

As the Postmaster General of America in 1763, Franklin installed an odometer (also known as a way-wiser) in his touring carriage during a five-month journey to examine postal routes. The odometer worked by

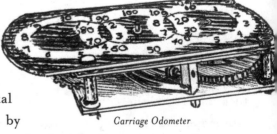

Carriage Odometer

measuring revolutions of a carriage wheel with a known circumference. This allowed Franklin to calculate distances and plan more direct and efficient routes. One of the first odometers dates back to 27 to 32 A.D. as described by Marcus Vitruvius Pollio, a Roman engineer, architect, and writer.

★ FRANKLIN FONETIC ★

Ben Franklin, as a gifted writer and accomplished printer, also took to tinkering with the mechanics of the English language as well. Ben felt that the alphabet needed some improvements and should be reconfigured to work phonetically. He eliminated six letters that he felt were redundant and, thus, should be cut from that cast of 26 characters. He decided that the characters of c, j, q, w, x, and y had to go. To take their place, he introduced a series of six ligature-like characters that represented phonetic sounds of specific letter pairings.

a b c d e f g h i j k l m n o p q r s t u v w x y z

Benjamin Franklin's new and "improved" alphabet, the Franklin Fonetic, eliminated six letters from the standard alphabet including c, j, q, w, x, and y.

Franklin wrote a new treatise in 1768 to promote his new phonetic alphabet, "A Scheme for a new Alphabet and a Reformed Mode of Spelling" (later published in his collected *Political, Miscellaneous, and Philosophical Pieces* in 1779). He then designed the new letter-forms to represent his new characters and had the type cast into lead for the printing press.

There wasn't a whole lot of interest in Ben's new alphabet, so the idea eventually went by the wayside. Noah Webster (of the legendary *Webster's Dictionary*) did take up the cause to distinguish American English from British English and separate it into a language all its own. Americans, however, were resistant to the notion, so Mr. Webster stuck to defining words rather than the alphabet.

NEW CHARACTERS	
LETTER	PRONUNCIATION KEY
a	(*aw*) John, folly; Awl, ball
y	(*uh*) um, un; as in umbrage, unto
ħ	(*sh*) ship, wish
ŋ	(*ng*) ing, reporting, among
h	(*th*) think
ħ	(*dh*) thy

★ STUDIES AT SEA ★

Benjamin Franklin had developed an "inclination toward the sea" in his youth, so his natural interest in it also led him to train his keen mind to investigate mysteries that had intrigued him during his transoceanic journeys. During his various voyages he would take the opportunity to test the waters, so to speak.

It was in 1768 that Franklin, as Deputy Postmaster of the American Colonies, decided he would try to identify a peculiarity that had mystified seafarers for centuries. He would undertake a serious enquiry into why packet ships took two to three weeks longer when traveling to America than when they traveled to Europe. Franklin had discussed the phenomenon with his cousin Timothy Folger, a Nantucket whaler, and the two worked on the problem.

Ben first began noting this oddity on the return leg of his first trip to London in 1726. He determined that there was a distinguishable separation in the water that indicated a difference in the color and temperature of the water as well as the sea tangles afloat in it. This seemed to indicate that there was something like a river in the ocean. Franklin had continued to record his observation and measurements in a journal during his transatlantic voyages. Folger, likewise, had considered and thought about the nature of this possible "river" in the Atlantic and had noted that patterns of whale traffic that tended to follow its course.

In 1769-1770, Franklin and Folger produced a map that provided a clear picture of the course of this oceanic current that Ben would call the Gulf Stream. The map that the two produced was remarkably accurate and has stood the test of time. Their map has been further refined in its findings, but has never been disputed — even as much more sophisticated technology-driven methods of mapmaking have evolved.

The Gulf Stream is a transoceanic current that originates in the Gulf of Mexico and follows the North American eastern seaboard from Florida to Newfoundland before forking into the Irminger Current (which flows toward Iceland), the North Atlantic Current (which flows toward the British Isles), and the Canary Current (which flows toward

West Africa). The Gulf Stream is essentially a massive river of warm water that is approximately fifty-six miles wide and travels at a speed greater than five knots at its peak velocity. The Gulf Stream reportedly channels more water than all of the rivers of the world combined.

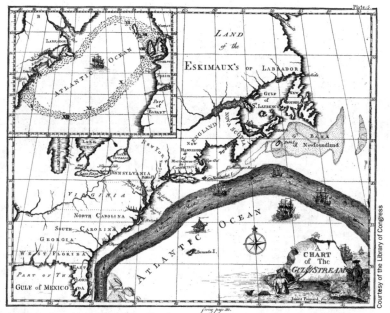

Engraver James Poupar of Philadelphia created this 1786 map based on maps made by Benjamin Franklin and Timothy Folger.

Ben also applied his mind to other marine matters during his travels and proposed a number of innovations. These included a more efficient sail array to reduce drag and enhance ship propulsion, a sea anchor for use in rough seas, the concept of double-hulled vessels, and numerous other improvements to sea travel.

★ COLD CASE ★

In 1773, Ben observed that the common cold was not a result of being exposed to cold weather — but rather more directly — as an interpersonal infection. There is a famed incident wherein Ben Franklin and John Adams found themselves sharing a night's lodging and a discourse on Franklin's observation.

Adams was deathly afraid of the chill night air and insisted that the window of the room be closed to avoid catching a cold. Franklin threw the window back open and jumped into bed. He then went about the task of educating Adams about his theories of "transpiration" at length. As Franklin droned on and on, Adams ultimately forgot about the frigid night air and drifted off to sleep.

Franklin, seemingly never tired of the subject himself, would state in a letter to Dr. Benjamin Rush in July of that same year:

> I have long been satisfy'd from Observation, that besides the general Colds now termed *Influenza's*, which may possibly spread by Contagion as well as by a particular Quality of the Air, People often catch Cold from one another when shut up together in small close Rooms, Coaches, &c. and when sitting near and conversing so as to breathe in each others Transpiration, the Disorder being in a certain State.

In fact, Franklin believed that circulated air was one of the best natural preventatives for disease. He would often take air-baths (and if he had neglected to leave the curtains sashed, his neighbors would be in for quite a show). He would let the breezes of refreshing and bracing cold air cleanse him of impurities.

Franklin would write to French physician Jacques Barbeu-Dubourg in 1768 of his air-bath ritual:

> I rise early almost every morning and sit in my chamber, without any clothes whatever, half an hour or an hour, according to the season, either reading or writing.

★ BALLOON BALLYHOO ★

On August 27, 1783, Ben was on hand in Paris to witness one of the earliest air flights of a man-made object. The first hydrogen-filled balloon flight — which Franklin had contributed funds to — took to the skies with great fanfare, launched by Jacques-Alexandre-Cesar Charles. This trek into the wild blue yonder created a sensation, with 50,000 or so cheering French citizens watching the silk balloon ascend to some 3,000 feet.

The Charles balloon voyage, however, did end with some embarrassment when the descending balloon was attacked and destroyed by frightened peasants on its return to the Earth in a village some 15 miles from Paris.

Later that year, Ben was also present to witness yet another history-making journey into the skies over Paris. Two brothers from Annonay in southern France, Joseph and Etienne Montgolfier, had developed an alternative method for the inflation of an air-faring balloon: hot air. Their balloon, the Montgolfière, first took flight on June 4, 1783. It then made a handful of test flights as they continued to perfect their creation.

November 21 became the day that would forever change man's relationship with gravity. Jean-Francois Pilâtre de Rozier and Francois Laurent, the Marquis d'Arlandes — the very first human aeronauts — piloted the Montgolfière to a height of 3,000 feet over Paris and traveled about six miles into the countryside (the two men had been preceded by the first animal aeronauts, including a sheep, duck, and rooster on a prior voyage of September 19 at Versailles).

Franklin, as a prominent scientific figure of the time, signed a document to certify the history-making voyage the following day at the request of the pioneering Montgolfier brothers. That day is still celebrated as Montgolfier Day in balloonist circles to recognize the remarkable accomplishment of that inaugural manned flight.

Ben believed that this mode of travel would "pave the way to some discoveries in natural philosophy of which at present we have no conception," as he would later tell Sir Joseph Banks, President of the Royal Society of London. When discussing the use and potential of balloon flight with a skeptic, Franklin retorted, "What is the use of a newborn baby?"

During Ben Franklin's days as an American ambassador to France in 1783, he was invited to face the "Turk" in a chess match in Paris. The Turk was a chess playing automaton (an early version of a robotic device). It was a sensation of the day where it played exhibition matches for the delight of the royalty of Europe in Vienna, Paris, Dresden, Leipzig, and London, among other cities, during its European tour.

Benjamin Franklin and Napoleon Bonaparte (who attempted to cheat in the first match) were among the luminaries who were defeated by the mechanical chess marvel.

The Turk was, in fact, an elaborate hoax. A concealed chess master controlled the Turk's moves from within a hidden compartment of the Turk's inner mechanisms.

While the Turk was a fake, Franklin's passion for chess was very real. He was an enthusiastic player and his essay, "The Morals of Chess," is highly regarded and quoted in chess circles to this day. Franklin was inducted into the U.S. Chess Hall of Fame in 1999.

★ DOUBLE VISION ★

In 1784, Franklin innovated with eyeglasses. He had difficulty seeing at a distance as well as up close with his aging eyes. He commissioned his optician to create lenses that would perform the double-duty of enabling sight at a distance as well as close-up without switching from spectacles to reading glasses.

The optician horizontally bisected the vision correcting lenses as well as magnifying lenses and mounted the two halves together into the lens frame of Franklin's spectacles. The two lenses which would correct his nearsightedness in the top half of the oval and a magnifying lens for reading or hand work in the bottom and, thus, bifocal glasses — or double spectacles as Franklin would call them — were born.

Ben's Bifocals

While serving as Ambassador to France in 1784, Benjamin Franklin was given a special assignment by the French Academy of Sciences at the request of King Louis XVI. A physician of some renown, Franz Anton Mesmer, had recently moved his practice from Vienna to Paris. A number of notables in the French court, including Queen Marie Antoinette as well as Wolfgang Amadeus Mozart, were counted among his supporters. Louis XVI was somewhat skeptical of Mesmer and his methods.

Mesmer claimed to be able to sense certain cosmic energies in the form of magnetic fluids that are part of all living things. He claimed that he was able to balance out these energies in an individual through his mastery of "Animal Magnetism." His method to induce a trance-like state involved some techniques that later evolved into the discipline of hypnotherapy. Mesmer even used the soothing sounds of Franklin's Glass Armonica as part of his treatment regime.

The commission, of which Ben was a member, conducted an investigation of mesmerism at Franklin's Paris residence. Dr. Charles d'Eslon took the battery of tests on behalf of Mesmer. The commission could not recognize any substantial evidence for the existence of Animal Magnetism. Mesmer was subsequently discredited and departed from Paris.

The infamous Franz Anton Mesmer

INNOVATOR AND INVENTOR:

A CHRONOLOGY

1717	Invents swim fins
1743	Founds American Philosophical Society
1744	Creates Pennsylvania Fireplace (later called the Franklin Stove)
1745	Begins electrical experiments
1750	Invents lightning rod
1751	Improved street lighting in Philadelphia with new lantern designs
	Experiments and Observations on Electricity, Made at Philadelphia in America published
	Invents lightning bells
	Conducts kite experiment
	Develops flexible urinary catheter
1753	Awarded Copley Medal by the Royal Society of London
	Awarded honorary degree from Harvard University
	Awarded honorary degree from Yale University
	Invented three-wheel clock
1759	Awarded honorary Doctor of Laws degree by University of St. Andrews
	Elected honorary member of the Philosophical Society of Edinburgh
1762	Invents Glass Armonica
	Awarded honorary Doctor of Civil Law degree from Oxford University
1763	Installs odometer into postal carriages
1768	Creates phonetic alphabet
	Charts Gulf Stream
1772	Elected member of French Academy of Sciences
1777	Elected member of Royal Medical Society of Paris
1783	Observes first hot air balloon flights in Paris
	Plays chess against the Turk, mechanical chess marvel
	Elected Honorary Fellow of Royal Society of Edinburgh
1784	Discredits Franz Anton Mesmer and Animal Magnetism
	Invents bifocals
	Proposes Daylight Savings Time in a satirical letter
1786	Invents long-arm (an instrument for retrieving books from high shelves)
1789	Elected member of Russian Imperial Academy of Sciences

Ben on the Bench
John Boyle, 1987

This sculpture, a gift from the Class of 1962, was donated to the University of Pennsylvania on the occasion of their 25th reunion. The friendly life-size statue invites passersby to take a seat next to the Penn founder Benjamin Franklin, as he reads from *The Pennsylvania Gazette*. The statue is located at 37th Street and Locust Walk on the Penn campus in Philadelphia.

PART FIVE

CITIZEN
and
STATESMAN

Franklin was an improver of self and surroundings. He applied this practice to that which he saw in the mirror and that which he saw around him. His active mind continually processed problems both practical and theoretical. This unique skill set contributed to his success as printer and writer as well as inventor and scientist.

He would use his knack for what would be known as out-of-the-box thinking and tinkered with the status quo. He applied unconventional solutions to conventional problems. Ben accomplished some of this good through his own single-mindedness in making a thing better. But he would also direct his extraordinary cleverness for the public good as well.

Benjamin Franklin engaged in numerous self-improvement endeavors. The most famed among these was his project for moral perfection.

He identified twelve virtues that he would focus on practicing. These virtues included temperance, silence, order, resolution, frugality, industry, sincerity, justice, moderation, cleanliness, tranquility, and chastity. A Quaker acquaintance suggested that he add just one more: humility, something Ben wasn't noted for.

He would concentrate on each virtue weekly, thereby completing four cycles of his thirteen virtues over the year. Any infractions would be recorded as black marks on the pages of a small booklet. Clean pages equaled clean living.

Diagram based on Ben's "book of virtue."

Ben would have areas of the day blocked off for specific tasks. For instance, one of the fundamental activities of the discipline of Order was the daily contemplation and consideration of "What good shall I do this day?" from 5:00 a.m to 12:00 p.m. each day.

Detail of embroidery on the sash said to have been Ben Franklin's while a member of the Lodge of the Nine Sisters in France.

There were some causes that were better served in concert with partners. He thus became a founder and joiner of groups. Ben began a club for industrious and upwardly mobile tradesmen in 1731 called the Junto. He also joined another group, the Freemasons, that same year. Franklin went on to form the Union Fire Company to protect people and property in 1736. He would also form an organization for the advancement of science, the American Philosophical Society, in 1743. And when circumstances called for it, he even organized a militia in 1747 and again in 1756.

Benjamin Franklin was very likely the smartest man in any given room he happened to enter. Yet there were instances where he found it wise to suppress his own contribution to a cause (and at times by way of writing anonymous tracts) in order to gather wider support — especially across the rigid societal class layers of the day.

In his youth, Ben was well aware of his great gifts and displayed that confidence. But as he grew older, he realized that it was best not to have one personality at the center of an initiative and thus would "wrap his talents in a napkin" by putting his ego aside for the greater good. This practice would

Benjamin Franklin was inducted into the American Mensa Hall of Fame in 1990. Mensa is a high IQ society whose membership scores in the top two percentile of standard IQ tests.

serve him well when working with the "better sort," and especially when he was a diplomat — both foreign and domestic — throughout his distinguished career.

Franklin would propose and publicize a number of public-spirited ventures that would make the lives of his fellow citizens better. These improvements would include the inventions of a more efficient heating stove, lifesaving lightning rods, and bifocal spectacles (all for which he chose to forgo potentially profitable patents). Ben's civic generosity likewise extended to progress for the populace as a whole. This involved — among a number of public-minded endeavors — the improvement of Philadelphia streets as well as the founding of a library, a hospital, a fire department, a militia, a university, and, ultimately, a nation.

★ ALL FOR ONE, ONE FOR ALL ★

In 1731, Franklin began to assemble a group of like-minded ambitious young tradesman. He brought them into a semi-secret society dedicated to their mutual advancement as well as those around them. The Junto as it was called (but also known as the Leather Apron Club) met once a week.

Some of the society's original members included Hugh Meredith (Franklin's coworker at Samuel Keimer's printing firm and future business partner of Franklin), William Godfrey (for whom Franklin printed an almanac), Robert Grace (who would one day manufacture Franklin's famous stove), and George Webb (who would share the plans of Franklin and Meredith to publish a newspaper with Keimer).

Franklin remembered the gathering of this guild some years later in the pages of his autobiography:

> ... I had formed most of my ingenious acquaintance into a club of mutual improvement, which we called the JUNTO; we met on Friday evenings. The rules that I drew up required that every member, in his turn, should produce one or more queries on any point of Morals, Politics, or Natural Philosophy, to be discussed by the company; and once in three months produce and read an essay of his own writing, on any subject he pleased.

Benjamin Franklin was proud to be a tradesman and a "leather apron man."

Our debates were to be under the direction of a president, and to be conducted in the sincere spirit of inquiry after truth, without fondness for dispute, or desire of victory; and, to prevent warmth, all expressions of positiveness in opinions, or direct contradiction, were after some time made contraband, and prohibited under small pecuniary penalties.

★ LAUNCHING A LIBRARY ★

Franklin not only was a writer and printer of the written word in periodical and pamphlets, but he also had a great fondness for books that dated back to his boyhood. He wanted to share that passion with his fellow Philadelphians in his first public-spirited venture.

Ben founded the first successful lending library in the American colonies in 1731. The Library Company of Philadelphia began as a subscription library among Franklin and members of the Junto. Library Company subscribers would contribute an initiation fee and an annual contribution that would fund the purchase of a collection of books that none of the members could acquire separately.

Franklin remarked that the library "improved the general conversation of the Americans" and was an equalizing force that provided the opportunity to tradesmen to become as learned as their social "betters."

The Library grew far beyond Franklin and his circle of friends. It served as the Library of Congress from the 1770s to 1800 while Philadelphia was the nation's capitol. The Library also became the largest lending library in the United States until the 1850s. The Library Company of Philadelphia still operates to this day as the oldest library in the United States. It is an independent research library specializing in the American culture of the seventeenth through nineteenth centuries.

★ FLAME FOILER ★

"Keep the home fires burning" has long been a popular sentiment evocative of the warmth and security of hearth and home. Benjamin Franklin was a great proponent of keeping those fires contained and controlled in the home. Firstly, Franklin had created a more efficient means of heating homes with his Pennsylvania Fireplace. And he would also advise that "an ounce of prevention is worth a pound of cure" in recommendations for the proper handling of hot coals and fireplace implements as well as proper chimney maintenance in the pages of *The Pennsylvania Gazette* and in other writings.

Ben had additionally founded the Union Fire Company on December 7, 1736 with some thirty other volunteers, many of whom were also members of the Junto. The Union Fire Company required that its members have leather buckets and strong bags at the ready and arrive quickly to the scene of a fire. When the company wasn't fighting fires together, they met monthly for lessons and discussions on fire fighting as well as for manly camaraderie. The Union Fire Company (which was also known as Benjamin Franklin's Bucket Brigade) proved to be a model that was

Fireman Franklin

followed with the establishment of a number of fire companies throughout Philadelphia.

Some years later, Franklin would introduce yet another new notion to Philadelphia in 1752 as a founder of the Philadelphia Contributionship for the Insurance of Houses from Loss by Fire. Fire insurance had first originated in Britain, and that concept must have inspired Franklin in the formation of Philadelphia's first and America's oldest property insurance company.

Insured buildings displayed a "fire mark" to alert fire fighters of their priority status.

★ PROMOTING USEFUL KNOWLEDGE ★

The physical sciences were regarded in the realm of "natural philosophy" in Colonial America. A number of learned men in the gentry aspired to be "natural philosophers" and were keenly interested in studying the physical sciences. As Benjamin Franklin wrote in 1743, "There are many in every Province in Circumstances that set them at Ease, and afford Leisure to cultivate the finer Arts, and improve the common Stock of Knowledge."

Those words were part of a pamphlet Ben wrote entitled *A Proposal for Promoting Useful Knowledge* among the British Plantations in America. Creating pamphlets for causes would become a successful strategy for Franklin, who would put his wizardry with words in making the case. This particular pamphlet made the argument and created support for the formation of an organization dedicated to the advancement of knowledge.

Courtesy of the Library of Congress

The American Philosophical Society, founded in 1743, would count among its membership such luminaries as George Washington, Thomas Jefferson, Thomas Paine, John Audubon, Charles Darwin, Thomas Edison, and Albert Einstein. The Society, headquartered in Philadelphia, is still a dynamic force for the promotion of useful knowledge to this day.

★ POLITICS AND PUBLIC POSTS ★

Franklin's first forays into the realm of public service were not exactly entirely out of benevolence, but began as a journey that was guided by enlightened self-interest. The intersection of Franklin's commercial interests and his involvement with useful endeavors for the betterment of society gained him influential friends. As a printer, Ben was well aware that the steadiest stream of revenue came from government printing contracts.

By impressing the Pennsylvania General Assembly in 1729 with their own version of an address of the Governor that had previously been published by Andrew Bradford, Franklin and partner Hugh Meredith succeeded in both exhibiting their superior workmanship as well as showing up their competition. This deed gained the interest of the Assembly and Franklin's printing business gradually obtained more business with the Commonwealth of Pennsylvania (which led to business with other colonial governments as well).

Benjamin Franklin was appointed to Clerk of the Pennsylvania General Assembly in 1736. Franklin had been seeking this opportunity to strengthen his ties to the legislature and gain additional printing work for the Commonwealth of Pennsylvania.

Ben was awarded with another political appointment in 1737, when he became postmaster of Philadelphia. The position of postmaster was a great

Ben didn't find the job requirements of the Clerk of the Pennsylvania General Assembly very challenging. He may have been bored with the duties required of him in this post, but he did find a novel way of passing the time during the tedium of Assembly proceedings. A mathematical game that he devised of "magic squares," in fact, has stood the test of time far longer than any of his work as Clerk of the Assembly.

The "magic square" configuration was an eight-by-eight block grid of numbers (see example below) representing the following conditions:

Each row and column of numbers added up to a constant of 260.

Each series of the first or second set of four numbers in each row or column would add up to 130.

Each grouping of four squares would total 130.

The numbers in each of the four corners plus the center cluster of four would also equal 260.

The main "bent diagonals"—which were the four squares extending diagonally toward the center from each corner and then arcing back along the four squares diagonally toward the corner horizontally opposite from the originating corner—also equaled the sum of 260.

52	61	4	13	20	29	36	45
14	3	62	51	46	35	30	19
53	60	5	12	21	28	37	44
11	6	59	54	43	38	27	22
55	58	7	10	23	26	39	42
9	8	57	56	41	40	25	24
50	63	2	15	18	31	34	47
16	1	64	49	48	33	32	17

advantage to a printer and newspaperman in that day and age. Whether or not a newspaper could be distributed by mail was sometimes the decision of the local postmaster. Andrew Bradford, publisher of the *American Weekly Mercury*, had been the postmaster of Philadelphia before Franklin. He had placed obstacles to the distribution of Franklin's *Pennsylvania Gazette*. Franklin, to his credit, did not treat Bradford similarly when the job became his. Ben would later be named Joint Postmaster General for the Crown in 1753 and ultimately would become the postmaster for the United Colonies in 1775.

Ben threw his hat into the political arena and took a more active role in public service in 1748 with his election to the Common Council of Philadelphia. Elections were a very different thing in the eighteenth century than they are in the modern day. One said he was available for office, rather than running for it. It was unseemly for a gentleman to seek an office; instead, it was better for an elected office to come to them. A candidate's most dignified trait was his lack of interest in being a politician — which is a far cry from the contemporary media age of fame-hungry office seekers.

Franklin thought his dedication to the common good through civic service a worthy pursuit for a recently retired gentleman and that it brought him honor and distinction. Ben's business in the public interest broadened with the office of justice of the peace, to which he was named in 1748. The year 1751 brought a new elected honor to Franklin when he became an assemblyman in the Pennsylvania General Assembly (a seat which he would hold until 1764, the year that he would be Speaker of that body). Franklin would then be voted into office as a Philadelphia alderman (member of city council) in 1764 after leaving the Assembly.

The political career of Benjamin Franklin would also consist of a number of appointments. These included being a colonial agent for Pennsylvania, Massachusetts, Georgia, and New Jersey.

Franklin's final governmental post was president of the Supreme Executive Council (which was relatively equivalent to being the governor) of the Commonwealth of Pennsylvania from 1785 to 1788.

★ A YEARNING FOR HIGHER LEARNING ★

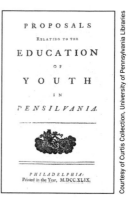

Benjamin Franklin published an anonymous pamphlet in 1749 called *Proposals Relating to the Education of Youth in Pennsylvania.* He wrote the pamphlet to create interest in an institution of higher learning in Philadelphia that was focused more on the liberal arts and less in religious education. This difference would make the new school distinct from other American colleges including Harvard University (founded 1636), the College of William and Mary (founded 1693), Yale University (founded 1701), and Princeton University (founded 1746).

Franklin succeeded in his goal of building public support for the project. He then took on the task of putting together a number of notable Philadelphians and raising money for the founding of what would become the world-renowned University of Pennsylvania.

Originally known as the Academy of Philadelphia, the college opened in 1751 on Fourth and Arch Streets. The Academy would be later called the College of Philadelphia in 1755. In 1779 it was then renamed as the University of the State of Pennsylvania. Ultimately, the institution would be known as the University of Pennsylvania in 1791. It would establish America's first medical school (University of Pennsylvania School of Medicine, 1765), business school (The Wharton School, 1881), and law school (Penn Law, 1790). The University, widely referred to as Penn, is now located in the heart of the University City district in Philadelphia.

It seems that rivalries between academic institutions extend beyond reputations, rankings, and athletic competitions. A number of these institutions have backdated their beginnings in order to be considered among the first founded.

The University of Pennsylvania had redefined in 1899 its date of founding back to 1740 (although it officially opened in 1751). The College of William and Mary has also sought to shift its founding date to 1693, although classes commenced in 1701 (but also claims its roots may reach even further back to 1618). Yale University was founded in 1701 (but traces its origins backward to the 1640s).

★ HAWKING FOR A HOSPITAL ★

Benjamin Franklin's affinity for public promotion was also put to good use in the campaign to establish a house of healing for the poor and the sick in Philadelphia in 1751. Dr. Thomas Bond enlisted the aid of his friend Franklin to gather support for the establishment of what would be America's first hospital.

Ben began advocating for the funding and founding of the institution. His efforts were resisted by the Pennsylvania General Assembly. Members of the Assembly representing areas outside of the city argued that this measure only helped Philadelphia and wasn't in their interest.

Franklin proposed a compromise measure with which he was able to get approval from the Assembly. The idea was that if he were to raise £2000, then the Province of Pennsylvania would contribute £2000 to the cause. This form of fundraising would become known as the matching grant, yet another Franklin innovation.

Ben would one day write in his autobiography of the founding of the Pennsylvania Hospital:

A convenient and handsome building was soon erected; the institution has by constant experience been found useful, and flourishes to this day; and I do not remember any of my political maneuvers, the success of which gave me at the time more pleasure, or wherein, after thinking of it, I more easily excused myself for having made some use of cunning.

Pennsylvania Hospital

Today, the Pennsylvania Hospital is part of the University of Pennsylvania Health System.

★ JOIN, OR DIE ★

The summer of 1754 was a crucial moment in the foundation of what would later be called "a more perfect union." Representatives for the colonies of New York, Connecticut, Massachusetts, New Hampshire, New Jersey, Pennsylvania, and Maryland met in upstate New York for the Albany Congress.

This gathering was held at the direction of British officials. They had recommended that the colonies create a centralized authority that would devise a universal set of policies about dealing with Native Americans and other items related to the common interests and common defense of the thirteen colonies. The moment was right to build a united front as the interests of the American Colonials, English, French, and the various Native American nations were colliding. Conflict was brewing, and the French and Indian War was on the near horizon.

The French and Indian War (also called the Seven Years War or the War of the Conquest) took place between 1754 and 1763. This conflict on North American soil was primarily about territorial expansion and the competing interests of the French and British (as well as the Spanish) empires in the New World of the Americas.

The French joined with Native American tribes, whose land was being increasingly invaded by the British and Colonial Americans. The British as well as Colonial American militia and their own Native American allies fought against the forces pushing back as they moved outward into the frontier.

The British ultimately won as the hostilities drew to a close. The power of the British empire in North America was ensured. One of the outcomes of this struggle was the heavy financial burden imposed on Great Britain in her effort to defend and increase the United Kingdom's possessions in North America. In time, oppressive taxes and duties were imposed on the American colonies in an attempt to pay for the expenses of the British defense of the American colonies.

It later became apparent how American colonists felt about taxation without representation — and how an enemy of one's enemy would become one's friend, as France would be a new friend in America.

Franklin had circulated the idea of a centralized body that would address these concerns for some time. The news of an upcoming gathering for this purpose inspired Franklin to create the enduring "Join, or Die" image (which, as was noted earlier, has earned the distinction of being the first American editorial cartoon as published in the May 9, 1754 *Pennsylvania Gazette*). Franklin publicly identified himself as a powerful proponent of this initiative. He was subsequently appointed by the Pennsylvania General Assembly to join the caucus.

The Albany Congress began its work on June 19, 1754. A plan that Benjamin Franklin drafted became the one that the conference would put forth as its final recommendation on July 10, 1754. The Albany Plan of Union became one of the earliest blueprints for the framework for American independence.

The British government ultimately dismissed the plan. It concluded that it went too far in creating a strong executive power that could prove difficult to manage and could potentially challenge British authority.

Courtesy of the Library of Congress

The colonies also rejected the plan. They believed it gave too much power to a single political body that could potentially infringe on the liberties of individual colonies. This rejection revealed an independent streak that would resurface during the Federalist/Anti-Federalist clashes when drafting the Constitution in 1791.

Some of the concepts Franklin backed in this landmark document would become part of the framework of the Articles of Confederation drafted almost two dozen years later in 1777.

The Federalist versus Anti-Federalist debate was principally between supporters of the formation of a strong central government (notably Alexander Hamilton, James Madison, and John Jay) and those who were in favor of individual state sovereignty (led by Patrick Henry).

Read more about the road to the Constitution of the United States of America in Part Six, pp. 128-132.

★ MILITARY MAN ★

The frontier was a dangerous place in the 1750s. As settlers moved outward from major population centers, they clashed with the Native Americans who lived in those outlying areas. As previously noted, some of the Native American tribes joined with the French in the battle for territory in North America. As confrontations became more commonplace, there appeared to be a need to strengthen the defense of the American Colonial frontier and deal with these escalating engagements.

British General Edward Braddock and two regiments were sent to remove French and Indian enemies along the western frontier from Pennsylvania to Ohio to New York to Ontario. Benjamin Franklin met with Braddock and his forces in the spring of 1755 for the purpose of planning a supply route for their use. He learned that provisions, including wagons and horses, were not readily available for Braddock's troops.

Franklin helped the mission further by putting out word about the shortness of supplies for the soldiers. He subsequently became a guarantor for the purchase of sufficient resources from private citizens. Fortunately for Franklin, the general was sent the money needed to compensate the owners of the wagons and horses before they began their journey westward.

Benjamin Franklin: Printer, Author, Inventor, Public Servant — and Soldier?

General Braddock made the classic mistake of underestimating his enemy. He suffered a devastating defeat by the French at their base of Fort Duquesne (at modern day Pittsburgh, PA) on July 9, 1755. Braddock's forces were routed and the General soon after died from wounds sustained there. One of Braddock's soldiers, Lieutenant Colonel George Washington, was fortunate to escape the General's unhappy fate.

With these continuing battles on the frontier, the defense of Pennsylvanians became a priority. An effort was made to build and equip a military force (which was certainly the aim of the Albany Plan of Union). But there were two problems that proved an obstacle to this endeavor. The proprietors of Pennsylvania, the Penn family, argued that their properties were not subject to taxation and that they would not contribute to this cause. Also, the majority of pacifistic Quakers in the Pennsylvania General Assembly objected to spending public funds for military purposes.

Continuing attacks on the frontier moved both the Penn proprietors and the Quakers to reconsider their positions. Assemblyman Franklin was then able to pass bills in the Assembly for the establishment of a militia as well as a means to fund it. The bills passed just one day after the November 24, 1755 massacre in Gnadenhütten, Pennsylvania, which was carried out by French-allied Delaware Indians. The supply bill provided £55,000 from the Assembly. It would be in addition to a pledge of a £5,000 "gift" from the Penn proprietors. (The proprietor's generosity was in fact a shell game. They extracted that generous sum from frontier landholders by way of rents on properties.)

Delaware (also known as the Lenápe or "The People") Indians were of three distinct tribes. These included the Munsee (also known as the "wolf" tribe), the Unami (the "turtle" tribe), and the Unalachtigo (the "turkey" tribe). The tribes lived primarily along the Delaware River in areas of present-day New York, New Jersey, Pennsylvania, and Delaware.

Certainly one of the chief complaints and grievances of Native Americans was, of course, the theft of lands through bent and broken treaties. A prime example of that would be the "Walking Purchase" agreement with Pennsylvania's proprietors. The accord between the Penns and the Lenápe was based on a 1686 deed (reportedly of doubtful authenticity) that agreed to sign over in the sale as much land as a man could walk in a day-and-a-half. The agreement was corrupted by the fact that the Penns employed a team of three highly skilled runners. They made the walk into a distance race that resulted in the sole finisher covering 65 miles as opposed to the 40 miles that the Lenápe had presumed.

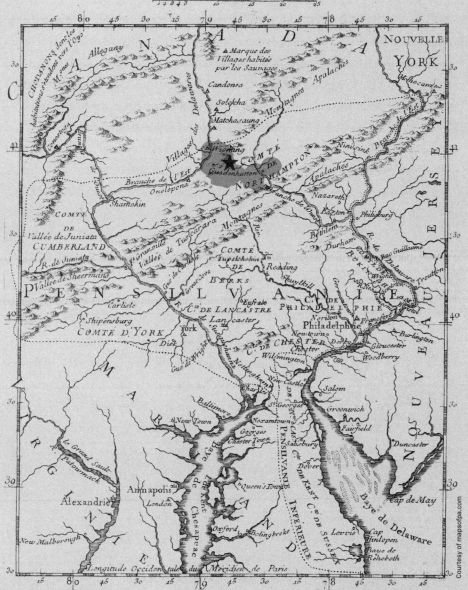

CARTE DE LA PENSILVANIE

Echelle de 25 Lieues comunes de France faisans 69 Milles Anglois.

Map of Southeastern Pennsylvania and the site of Gnadenhütten.

Chief Teedyuscung (known as the "King of the Delawares") of the Munsee Tribe led a raiding party of Delaware as well as a number of Shawnee and Mohican Indians that destroyed the Moravian mission village of Gnadenhütten (German for "Tents of Grace") on November 24, 1755. The mission at Gnadenhütten — which is present-day Lehighton, Pennsylvania — was home to sixteen white missionaries and about seventy Indian converts to Christianity. Ten of the sixteen missionaries were killed and most of the Indian converts were permitted to leave unhurt.

Benjamin Franklin, accompanied by his son William as his aide de camp, went on to Bethlehem, Pennsylvania, at the request of Pennsylvania Governor William Denny. The governor asked him to build a force and fortify the frontier to prevent further attack. Franklin raised a company of men for this purpose and built a fort and outposts in nearby Gnadenhütten and the surrounding area. And when military companies in Colonial America elected their officers, Benjamin Franklin could count the rank of colonel among his many accomplishments.

Ben's business of building a fighting force was not without precedent. He had made a powerful case in 1747 to persuade a company of 600 Philadelphia "gentlemen and merchants" to come together to form a voluntary militia through an anonymous pamphlet (attributed to "A Tradesman of Philadelphia") with the title *Plain Truth*.

Crest of the Associators of the City and Liberties of Philadelphia, from a 1748 design by Benjamin Franklin.

The Associators of the City and Liberties of Philadelphia organized in 1747 (and established the foundation for the Pennsylvania National Guard and today's 111th Infantry and 103rd Engineers) for the defense of Philadelphia from privateers on the Delaware River as well as French and Indian attacks. Because the Quaker-controlled Pennsylvania General Assembly was opposed to allocating funds for armed forces, Franklin created a lottery to pay for the Associators' supplies and munitions.

The public acclaim for this enterprise is said to have helped propel Franklin to elected office and into the Common Council of Philadelphia.

3d PHILADELPHIA LOTTERY.
1748. CLASS the Third. No. 2103
This Billet entitles the Bearer to such Prize as may be drawn against its Number in the third Class (if demanded within Six Months after the last Drawing is finished) subject to no Deduction if under Twenty Pieces of Eight.

Courtesy of the Historical Society of Pennsylvania

Ticket from Franklin's lottery system, devised to fund Philly's fighting forces.

A privateer is a privately owned ship and crew that are working as mercenaries for another government, typically attacking and capturing ships associated with the enemies of their employers.

★ ON THE STREETS OF PHILADELPHIA ★

Ben had been annoyed by the dust and debris kicked up from Philadelphia's dirt streets that was continually tracked into his shop and home. He consulted with his neighbors and they agreed to collectively hire a street sweeper.

This experience inspired a public initiative to pay for the paving and lighting of the streets of Philadelphia. In 1756, Franklin had introduced a bill to the Pennsylvania General Assembly that would do just that. In this manner, Ben had proposed a popular public service with advantages that his fellow citizens would willingly pay a tax to support.

Franklin, the constant innovator, also proposed an improvement to Philadelphia's street lighting in the bill. Ben devised a four-paned design for the lamps, which provided better ventilation in the gaslight lamps than the standard glass globe imported from London. This ensured that the streetlights would be easier to clean and maintain and not so soon become grimy with soot common to the globe design.

Benjamin Franklin made the streets of Philadelphia cleaner, better lit — and safer.

A 1777 map of the City of Philadelphia, a place that Benjamin Franklin made better —
and a place that loves him back to this day.

CITIZEN AND STATESMAN:

A CHRONOLOGY

1727	Forms the Junto
1731	Joins the Freemasons
	Founds the Library Company of Philadelphia
1736	Appointed Clerk of the Pennsylvania General Assembly
	Organizes the Union Fire Company
1737	Appointed Postmaster of Philadelphia
1743	Founds the American Philosophical Society
1747	Organizes the Associators for the City and Liberties of Philadelphia
1748	Elected to the Common Council of Philadelphia
1749	Promotes the founding of the Academy of Philadelphia (later called the University of Pennsylvania)
	Appointed Justice of the Peace
1751	Cofounds the Pennsylvania Hospital
1752	Cofounds The Philadelphia Contributionship for the Insurance of Houses from Loss by Fire
1753	Appointed joint Deputy Postmaster General of North America
1754	Drafts and signs the Albany Plan of Union
1756	Elected Colonel of the militia he leads to Gnadenhütten, Pennsylvania
	Introduces bill into Pennsylvania General Assembly for street paving and cleaning as well as installation of street lights
1757	Named colonial agent for Pennsylvania
1762	Maps postal routes of the colonies
1764	Elected Speaker of the Pennsylvania General Assembly
1775	Appointed Postmaster General for the United colonies
1787	Franklin College founded, named in Franklin's honor

The sage Benjamin Franklin
holds forth among the 42 life-
size bronze statues of Founding
Fathers in Signers' Hall.
Signers' Hall is one of the
signature exhibits at the
National Constitution
Center, located at
525 Arch Street
in Philadelphia.

Benjamin Franklin
Studio EIS, 2003

PART SIX

FOUNDER
and
FRAMER

By the rude bridge that arched the flood,
Their flag to April's breeze unfurled;
Here once the embattled farmers stood,
And fired the shot heard 'round the world.
— Ralph Waldo Emerson, "Concord Hymn"

The shots that rang out in the Battles of Lexington and Concord on April 19, 1775, boomed loudly in pre-revolutionary America — and they reverberated clear across the Atlantic. This opening salvo of the American Revolution, fired by the ragtag militiamen of Massachusetts and New Hampshire, was aimed squarely at one target: the tyranny of King George III and a British presence that the American colonies could tolerate no longer.

The armed rebellion that would become known as the War for American Independence didn't happen overnight. It had long been simmering before the Boston Tea Party of December 16, 1773, and even before the bloodshed of the Boston Massacre of March 5, 1770. There was a chain of events that stretched as far back as two decades to where the seeds of revolution were sown.

Illustration based on a detail of Paul Revere's famous engraving.

Nothing about the outcome of American War of Independence was assured. In fact, only a minority of American colonists were in support of cutting ties with Britain at first. The Americans were fighting the best-equipped military and the finest fighting force in the world. If luck hadn't been on their side at a few key moments, events would have unfolded far differently than they had.

To be sure, breaking the bond between the American colonies and Great Britain weighed heavily on those who supported the cause of American liberty. The opening lines of a pamphlet by *Common Sense* author Thomas Paine, *The Crisis* of December 23, 1776, captured the inner turmoil that troubled so many Americans and effectively drew the battle lines between them:

> These are the times that try men's souls: The summer soldier and the sunshine patriot will, in this crisis, shrink from the service of his country; but he that stands by it now, deserves the love and thanks of man and woman.

Benjamin Franklin, too, was torn on this issue. At one time, his tendency would be to settle the differences between American and Briton that split one from the other. Franklin was a loyal English subject. He was dedicated to the expansion and welfare of the British empire. But all that would change on one day in January 1774 before the Privy Council in London.

Out of all of the brilliant leaders and eloquent spokesmen for the cause of liberty, Thomas Paine (1737–1809) fueled the flames in hearts that desired to be free. He spoke plainly and made the common sense case for an America free of royal tyranny in the pamphlet with the direct title of *Common Sense*.

Common Sense, first published anonymously in 1775 and with more than 100,000 copies sold, was the best-selling book of the eighteenth century.

Illustration based on the 1880 portrait by Auguste Millière.

Ben would later discuss the prospect of reaching an understanding in a July 20, 1776, letter to Lord Howe after the war had begun:

> Long did I endeavor with unfeigned and unwearied Zeal, to preserve from breaking, that fine and noble China Vase the British Empire: for I knew that being once broken, the separate Parts could not retain even their Share of the Strength or Value that existed in the Whole, and that a perfect Re-Union of those Parts could scarce even be hoped for.

Benjamin Franklin's role in the beginning of American democracy has earned him the title "Founding Father" (although some might say "Founding Grandfather" because of the age difference between Ben and other members of the Revolutionary generation). Franklin, in fact, is the only Founder to sign five of the founding documents of American Independence. These include the Albany Plan of Union (1754), the Declaration of Independence (1776), the Treaties of Amity and Commerce (1778), the Treaty of Paris (1783), and the Constitution of the United States of America (1787).

★ BOUND FOR LONDON TOWN ★

Benjamin Franklin returned to Great Britain in 1757. His return, however, would be under dramatically different circumstances than when he last walked the streets of London more than thirty years before in 1726. He was no longer the stranded boy on his journey to manhood. He was now an honored dignitary on the international scene. He was the world-renowned man of science and tamer of electrical fire.

This significant standing made him the person to represent the interests of the people of Pennsylvania as a colonial agent in London. Franklin would be at this task for five years before returning to Philadelphia in 1762.

Franklin brought his twenty-six-year-old son William with him on this voyage to England. Staying at home in Philadelphia were his daughter Sally and wife Deborah. (Deborah feared sea travel and refused to make the trip across the Atlantic.) In London, Ben took up residence at No. 7 Craven Street. There he made a home away from home with his landlady

Margaret Stevenson and her daughter Mary (or "Polly" as she was called).

Franklin was captivated by the sights and sounds of bustling London. He settled in and expanded upon the friendships he had developed with many of his transatlantic correspondents. He also made a made a number of new friends as he once again became acquainted to the modern metropolis of London.

A good deal of Ben's business here was to go before British officials and make the people of Pennsylvania's case against the province's proprietors, the Penn family. Franklin also later represented the interests of Georgia in 1768, New Jersey in 1769, as well as Massachusetts in 1771 when he once again

Benjamin Franklin's home-away-from-home was at No. 7 Craven Street, now No. 36 Craven Street in today's London. In 2006 it was rechristened as the Benjamin Franklin House, a museum honoring its most famous resident. (See p. 154 for more about the Benjamin Franklin House.)

made an extended trip to London from 1765 and 1775. His principal mission during this period was to oppose the Penns and their power over Pennsylvania (specifically, to convert the charter for the colony to make it a royal colony, removing it from the ownership of the Penns).

★ STAMP OF DISAPPROVAL ★

Great Britain had spent considerable blood and treasure in defending her North American territories and the American colonies in the French and Indian War. After that war came to an end in 1763, the British Parliament wanted to make the colonists share some of that financial burden.

Beginning in 1764, the American Revenue Act was introduced (also known as the Sugar Act). This act introduced a new tax. This tax was actually lower than the one set in 1733 on sugar and molasses (key ingredients in the making of rum). However, the new tax was more vigorously enforced to raise revenue as well as discourage smuggling. The act also imposed taxes on the importation of coffee, wines, and other items. The export of lumber and iron was also regulated by this act.

The Stamp Act as introduced in this 1765 pamphlet set the Crown and the colonies on a collision course.

The British Parliament next passed the Currency Act, which regulated the currency system of the colonies. A few months later, the Parliament passed another financial act that affected the daily affairs of the colonists. The Stamp Act became law on February 16, 1765. Taxes were imposed by requiring colonists to purchase a government stamp for any official or legal document. Stamps also had to be purchased for essentially anything printed: pamphlets, periodicals, playing cards, and even dice.

This tax had the greatest impact on lawyers, printers, and merchants. And these were just the sort who were most inclined and most situated to howl loudly with protest. "No taxation without representation" henceforth became the rallying cry for the colonials from that point on.

Resistance soon began among those suffering from this heavy-handed tax. For example, *The Pennsylvania Gazette* — published by Franklin's business partner, David Hall — ran with a headline that read "No Stamped Paper to be had" on November 7, 1765. The newspaper additionally omitted the publication's masthead as a means to avoid the new law. Hall would continue to print the paper in this manner for some six weeks until December 26, 1765.

Franklin — who was in far-off London at the time — was not aware of the antagonism to the Stamp Act. In fact, many back home thought that Ben was engaged in the act's enactment. They mobbed his Philadelphia house and threatening to pull it down. Only the steadfast (and armed) Deborah Franklin was able to hold off the attack and save the Franklin homestead.

Ben was brought before the House of Commons in February 1766. He was asked to testify about the cause of the colonists' anger and how it might be alleviated. He spoke confidently and told the members of that body that the American colonists would not accept internal taxes such as the Stamp Act. They would, he said, find external taxes acceptable (typically indirect import duties). This would ultimately turn out to be completely wrong and a grave misreading of his countrymen's inclinations. The Stamp Act was subsequently repealed on March 8, 1766.

The British Parliament, however, was on a mission. It still needed to find a way to replenish the treasury and gain some control of these increasingly quarrelsome colonials. What followed was a flood of bills. These included the Quartering Act (March 1765), Declaratory Act (March 1766), the Townshend Revenue Act (June 1767), the Tea Act (May 1773), and the Intolerable Acts (March-June 1764).

★ THE CASE OF THE PURLOINED LETTERS ★

Benjamin Franklin had always been cautious in his dealings and affairs. But he made a serious miscalculation in a matter that would change his relationship with the British government. A number of letters addressed to the recently deceased Thomas Whatley (1726-1772) had come into his possession. These letters were originally from Governor Thomas Hutchinson (1711-1780) and Lieutenant Governor Andrew Oliver (1706-1774) of Massachusetts and were of an extremely sensitive nature.

Following the imposition of the Tea Act, Samuel Adams and his Sons of Liberty (some decked out as crude caricatures of Mohawk Indians) came to the Boston docks to dump some 342 chests (almost £100,000 worth) of tea into Boston Harbor on the cold night of December 16, 1773. The notorious dumping of the tea into the wintry waters of Boston Harbor would be infamously known as the Boston Tea Party thereafter.

The Intolerable Acts (more precisely: the Boston Port Act, the Administration of Justice Act, the Massachusetts Government Act, the Quartering Act of 1774, and the Quebec Act) were designed to be punitive and repressive. They followed directly on the heels of the Boston Tea Party.

Sam Adams (1722-1803) — cousin of John Adams — was a pivotal figure in the American Revolution, the fourth governor of Massachusetts, and the inspiration of the beer named in his honor. Illustration based on the 1772 portrait by John Singleton Copley.

This series of letters outraged Franklin. They advocated "an abridgment of what are called English liberties" for the unruly citizens of Massachusetts. Ben sent the letters to friends in Boston with explicit instructions to keep them confidential. Human nature being what it is (whether Franklin's directions were meant to be taken with a wink and a nod or not), the letters were soon published in the pages of *The Boston Gazette*.

This scheme was a turn at triangulation for Franklin. He placed the blame for the bad blood in Boston squarely on Governor Hutchinson. (Hutchinson had to flee back to Britain after the letters were published and the ensuing backlash.) Franklin tried to redirect any American hostility toward Britain back on Hutchinson with the release of the letters. Ben believed that reconciliation could be reached between the colonists and England by revealing Hutchinson's hypocrisy.

Franklin's involvement in the leaking of the letters was kept under wraps for a time. His role in the affair was later revealed when Franklin wrote of his deeds to the *London Chronicle* as a means to clear up a dangerous misunderstanding. He was moved to make his confessions after an inconclusive duel between Whatley's brother and another accused of stealing the letters (which was going to go into a rematch). Ben defended his actions as appropriate in that the contents of the letters were pertinent to the public interest of the people of Massachusetts. He maintained that these were not "private letters between friends" and thus should rightfully be made available for examination by the public.

It certainly wasn't seen that way when Franklin was called to appear before the British Privy Council in the Cockpit (the chamber earned its name because it was reportedly the site of cockfights during the reign of Henry VIII). After his initial appearance, Ben was allowed to have a lawyer represent him and return three weeks later to appear before the Council. He had no idea that the main focus of the proceedings would be entirely on his part in the publication of the personal letters of Hutchinson and Oliver. He had presupposed that the testimony would concentrate on the conduct of the Governor and Lieutenant Governor.

The public humiliation heaped upon Benjamin Franklin by Lord Alexander Wedderburn turned Franklin from friend to foe of the British empire.

Don't TREAD on me.

January 29, 1774, would prove to be a defining moment for Franklin and his national allegiance. On that day he stood before the Privy Council to answer for his actions. Ben endured unrelenting attacks by Lord Alexander Wedderburn (1733-1805), who hurled criticism and accusation at Franklin for his role in inciting insurrection among the colonists. Benjamin Franklin may have entered the Cockpit as an English subject seeking to repair the schism between England and her colonies. But when he left the Cockpit, he did so as an American.

Franklin was thoroughly tainted by these proceedings and any sort of rescue of his reputation in England was now impossible. And as further insult to injury, Ben was stripped of his post as Deputy Postmaster General of North America by the British government.

And then things got worse. Ben had been in London since December 1764 and had been working diligently to represent the interests of the colonies. The interests that should presumably have been his first priority — those of his family — didn't receive as much of his attention. Deborah Read Rogers Franklin suffered a severe stroke on December 14, 1774. She died a few days later on December 19. Ben hadn't been home to Philadelphia or seen his wife in just over ten years.

Franklin left London on March 20, 1775, and would arrive in an America that was already racing down the road of revolution in May 1775.

★ OUR SACRED HONOR ★

The April 19, 1775 Battles of Lexington and Concord had begun the hostilities and the shooting war between the American colonies and Great Britain. There were, however, other sparks of conflict that ignited between the combatants. The two sides clashed when circumstances would put them in one another's path. The Boston Massacre in March 1770 and the Gaspée Affair of June 1772 (wherein a British schooner was run aground by the Sons of Liberty) were such collisions.

The Second Continental Congress convened on May 10, 1775. It would coordinate and manage the American war effort. It would also act as a centralized government of the colonies in confronting the British. Presided over by John Hancock, the Second Continental Congress also debated the more contentious issues surrounding the colonies' long-term relations with their British brethren.

John Hancock (1737-1793), illustration based on the 1765 portrait by John Singleton Copley (1738-1815).

The Boston Massacre of March 5, 1770, was an infamous incident in which five Bostonians were killed after a crowd provoked a British sentry and the members of the regiment dispatched to come to his aid.

What followed was a flood of ill temper among the people of Boston as the English soldiers prepared for their prosecution. Unswayed by partisanship, John Adams — who would one day be a key character in the revolutionary drama and second president of the United States of America — stepped in as legal counsel. He successfully defended the soldiers in their trial for murder as a matter of law and justice.

The event would prove to be effective in the propaganda campaign of Samuel Adams (cousin to John Adams and leader of the Sons of Liberty). It stirred up the sentiments of the citizenry in support of their struggle against British rule. The etching by Paul Revere of the incident would prove to be a potent tool in the arsenal for this battle for hearts and minds on the home front.

John Adams, illustration based on the 1800 portrait by Gilbert Stuart (1755-1828).

background image: iStockphoto

By June 1776, it was apparent (even to those arguing for conciliation) that the united colonies must resolve to break their bonds with the United Kingdom. A committee from among the delegates to the Second Continental Congress was formed to write a formal declaration of this resolution. This committee included Pennsylvania's Benjamin Franklin, John Adams of Massachusetts, Thomas Jefferson of Virginia, Robert R. Livingston of New York, and Roger Sherman of Connecticut.

The committee members decided that the task of drafting the declaration should go to John Adams and Thomas Jefferson. Adams, in turn, asked Jefferson to take on the responsibility to be the principal writer. Jefferson was a Virginian — which was politically important — as well as a very gifted writer. Jefferson was also well liked among the delegates — at least better liked than the antagonistic Adams — which was also politically important.

The thirty-three-year-old Jefferson began writing on June 11 and continued his work until June 27. The work of Jefferson and the Declaration Committee was

Thomas Jefferson (1743-1826) went on to become the second governor of Virginia, the third president of the United States, and one of the most admired architects of American democracy (despite being a slave owner).

Illustration based on the 1821 portrait by Gilbert Stuart (1755-1828).

then examined by the larger body of the Congress as a whole, which debated the text from July 1 to July 4.

A number of edits during the process were made, which caused Thomas Jefferson considerable grief. One specific edit by Benjamin Franklin is particularly notable: In the original text, Jefferson had written that "We hold these truths to be sacred and undeniable, that all men are created equal." Franklin changed the phrase and "these truths" became the more humanistic "self-evident."

The document that Jefferson drafted, the Declaration of Independence, set forth principles of natural human rights. These principles became the cornerstone for that distinct nature of American freedom that would become the standard for liberty the world over. The impassioned case for American independence from Great Britain (including very specific grievances against King George III) began like this:

King George III (1738-1820) wasn't very popular in the American colonies.

In Congress, July 4, 1776.

A Declaration

By the Representatives of the United States of America, In General Congress assembled.

Illustration based on the 1762 portrait by Allan Ramsay (1713-1784).

When in the course of human Events, it becomes necessary for one People to dissolve the Political Bands which have connected them with another, and to assume among the Powers of the Earth, the separate and equal Station to which the Laws of Nature and of Nature's God entitle them, a decent Respect to the Opinions of Mankind requires that they should declare the causes which impel them to the Separation.

We hold these truths to be self-evident, that all men are created equal, that they are endowed by their Creator with certain unalienable rights, that among these are life, liberty and the pursuit of happiness. That to secure these rights, governments are instituted among men, deriving their just powers from the consent of the governed. That whenever any form of government becomes destructive to these ends, it is the right of the people to alter or to abolish it, and to institute new government, laying its foundation on such principles and organizing its powers in such form, as to them shall seem most likely to effect their safety and happiness. Prudence, indeed, will dictate that governments long established should not be changed for light and transient causes; and accordingly all experience hath shown that mankind are more disposed to suffer, while evils are sufferable, than to right themselves by abolishing the forms to which they are accustomed. But when a long train of abuses and usurpations, pursuing invariably the same object evinces a design to reduce them under absolute despotism, it is their right, it is their duty, to throw off such government, and to provide new guards for their future security.

The case for independence argued and powerfully stated, the Declaration closed with fortitude and resolve and in no uncertain terms:

> We, therefore, the Representatives of the united States of America, in General Congress, Assembled, appealing to the Supreme Judge of the world for the rectitude of our intentions, do, in the Name, and by Authority of the good People of these Colonies, solemnly publish and declare, That these united Colonies are, and of Right ought to be Free and Independent States, that they are Absolved from all Allegiance to the British Crown, and that all political connection between them and the State of Great Britain, is and ought to be totally dissolved; and that as Free and Independent States, they have full Power to levy War, conclude Peace, contract Alliances, establish Commerce, and to do all other Acts and Things which Independent States may of right do. — And for the support of this Declaration, with a firm reliance on the protection of Divine Providence, we mutually pledge to each other our Lives, our Fortunes, and our sacred Honor.

This proclamation of American emancipation, the Declaration of Independence, was adopted by the Second Continental Congress on July 4. It was printed as a broadside to commemorate the event. The Declaration was first officially read to the public on July 8.

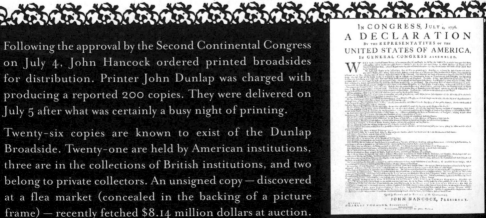

Following the approval by the Second Continental Congress on July 4, John Hancock ordered printed broadsides for distribution. Printer John Dunlap was charged with producing a reported 200 copies. They were delivered on July 5 after what was certainly a busy night of printing.

Twenty-six copies are known to exist of the Dunlap Broadside. Twenty-one are held by American institutions, three are in the collections of British institutions, and two belong to private collectors. An unsigned copy — discovered at a flea market (concealed in the backing of a picture frame) — recently fetched $8.14 million dollars at auction.

An enduring and popular misconception places all fifty-six signers at Independence Hall on the momentous day of July 4, 1776. There they are generally thought to have put their own "John Hancocks" to signify their support for the cause of independence. The delegates did officially adopt the Declaration on the Fourth of July, but the document was only officially signed on August 2, 1776, by the delegates in the Second Continental Congress. It took a few months for the remainder of the signers that were not present on that day to add their signatures to it.

Illustration (foreground figures, from left to right: John Adams, Roger Sherman, Robert Livingston, Thomas Jefferson, Benjamin Franklin, Charles Thomson, and John Hancock) based on the 1795 painting by John Trumbull (1756–1843).

With the inalienable right to life, liberty, and the pursuit of happiness thus asserted, the consequences of the approved text for the Declaration of Independence on July 4, 1776 certainly preyed on the mind of each and every one of the fifty-six men who signed it cannot be understated. The Signers made a solemn pledge to each other to stand together. They put their lives, fortunes — and most importantly — their sacred honor to a cause bigger than themselves.

Each of these fifty-six men who put pen to paper and endorsed this proclamation could just as easily have been signing their own death warrant. The punishment could be hanging for treason. John Hancock boldly put everything on the line with his signature. He is reported to have said at the official August 2 signing of the Declaration of Independence, "His majesty can now read my name without glasses. And he can also double the price on my Head. We must be unanimous; there must be no pulling different ways; we must all hang together."

John Hancock's famous signature has become iconic, and the act of writing one's signature remains as making your "John Hancock" in common parlance to this day.

Benjamin Franklin added, with no little irony and a touch of gallows humor, "We must all hang together, or assuredly we shall all hang separately."

★ A FRIEND OF FRANCE ★

Benjamin Franklin went to sea once more on October 27, 1776, and on the path across the Atlantic Ocean to Paris. Accompanied by two of his grandsons, William Temple Franklin (son of William Franklin) and Benjamin Franklin Bache (son of Sarah Franklin Bache), Franklin arrived in Paris on December 21, 1776. He was joined there by Arthur Lee and Silas Deane, who were to serve with Ben as appointed commissioners of the United States of America to forge an alliance with France.

The commissioners' business was to pursue a most favored nation status with France and to strengthen the hand of the Americans in their dealings with the English. The diplomacy practiced by the three commissioners as well as some encouraging successes on the battlefields back in the United States prompted the French to lend their support for the Americans' struggle for independence.

The Treaty of Amity and Commerce as well as the Treaty of Alliance were negotiated and ultimately signed in Paris on February 6, 1778. These two pacts would give the new American nation a powerful financial and military ally. Without their French ally, it was highly unlikely that the Americans would ultimately win their freedom from the British.

Benjamin Franklin not only rebelled against English authority, but against French fashion as well. Ben's insistence on dressing like an backwoods rustic (complete with beaver fur hat) really made him stand out on the streets of Paris.

Benjamin Franklin stood as a distinct figure in Paris, surrounded by French style and culture. He stood apart because of his unassuming manner and rugged individualism. He was also regarded as something of a celebrity, because of his breakthroughs in electricity. Ben Franklin represented a cultivated frontiersman from the far-flung American wilderness. He was a sylvan sage in the majesty of one of Europe's gleaming metropolises.

What was ultimately a nine-year stay in the Parisian suburb of Passy established Benjamin Franklin as a beloved figure among the French people. Franklin's face appeared everywhere in France — on medallions, busts, cameos, portraits, and engravings. He reported in a letter to his daughter, Sally, that "Your father's face is now as well known as the man in the moon."

However, not everyone in Paris adored Ben. Some of the greatest hostility he experienced came from his own countrymen and fellow commissioners: Silas Deane, Arthur Lee, and then John Adams.

On April 29, 1778, there was something of a sensation when Benjamin Franklin and the famed French philosopher Voltaire were urged to embrace in the French fashion on stage by an adoring audience at the Académie Royale. A jealous John Adams would write:

> Voltaire and Franklin were both present, and there presently arose a general cry that M. Voltaire and M. Franklin should be introduced to each other. This was done, and they bowed and spoke to each other. This was no satisfaction; there must be something more. Neither of our philosophers seemed to divine what was wished or expected. They, however, took each other by the hand; but this was not enough. The clamor continued until the exclamation came out, "Il faut s'embrasser à la Francaise!" ["(You must) kiss like the French kiss!"] The two aged actors upon this great theatre of philosophy and frivolity then embraced each other by hugging one another in their arms and kissing each other's cheeks, and then the tumult subsided. And the cry immediately spread throughout the kingdom, and I suppose over all Europe, "Qu'il etait charmant de voir embrasser Solon et Sophocle!" ["It was delightful to see Solon and Sophocles embrace!"]

Voltaire (1694–1778)

Illustration based on the 1778 bust by Jean-Antoine Houdon (1741–1828).

John Adams had replaced Silas Deane, who was asked to return to the United States. Adams wasn't so amused by the antics of "Mon Cher Papa" ["My Dear Papa"] — as the fashionable French ladies had called Ben. The forty-three-year-old Adams had mixed feelings about Franklin and held both veneration as well as venom for the elder statesman. He frequently seethed about Franklin's escapades. Adams would later write to Benjamin Rush (1746-1813) in 1790:

> The History of our Revolution will be one continued lie from one end to the other. The essence of the whole will be that Dr. Franklin's electric rod smote the earth and out sprang General Washington. Then Franklin electrified him... and thence forward those two conducted all the Policy, Negotiations, Legislations, and War.

The insecure John Adams felt over-shadowed amongst the larger-than-life figures that were his fellow Founders (chiefly Franklin, Washington, and Jefferson).

Illustration composition based on the cover of THOR #153 (June 1968) by Jack Kirby (1917-1994).

The commissioners had made plain their discontent with one another. They, along with the French, asked the Congress to do something about it. By February 1779, the Second Continental Congress had named Franklin the Sole Minister Plenipotentiary to France — and relieved Adams and Lee of their posts.

★ PEACE IN PARIS ★

The Battle of Yorktown, which lasted more than twenty days and ended on October 19, 1781, decisively concluded the American War of Independence militarily. General Lord Cornwallace's British forces were defeated by the combined might of the forces commanded by General George Washington and French General Comte de Rochambeau. But it took another two years to formally declare the hostilities at an end.

On September 3, 1783, Benjamin Franklin and fellow Commissioners John Adams and John Jay endorsed a treaty that would bring an official conclusion to the American Revolutionary War.

The Treaty of Paris — negotiated and signed in Paris — established that the thirteen colonies were sovereign and independent states. It also defined the boundaries of the United States of America. Other items agreed to in the Treaty of Paris included the release of prisoners and return of military property, the promised return of properties seized from Loyalists, the honoring of existing lawful contracts and obligations to creditors, the

Painter Benjamin West (1738-1820) embarked upon painting an epic scene capturing the event, but had only had the opportunity to paint the American contingent (including Benjamin Franklin, John Adams, John Jay, grandson William Temple Franklin, and Henry Laurens) since the British mediators refused to pose for the piece.

Reportedly, Ben was wearing the very same brown velvet suit at the signing ceremony that he wore the day of that January 29, 1774 blistering attack that he endured from Solicitor General Alexander Wedderburn before the English Privy Council in the Cockpit.

Illustration based on Benjamin West's 1783 painting.

granting of fishing rights in British Northern America, and free navigation of the Mississippi River by the United States of America and Great Britain.

The new North American map (at least east of the Mississippi River) after the signing of the Treaty of Paris.

One of the concessions that Franklin pushed for during the peace negotiations was the British ceding of the British North American territories and the transfer of Canada to the United States. This would seem to be an early expression of what would become known as Manifest Destiny in the figurative unfurling of the cloth that is America over the whole of the North American continent.

It wasn't the first time that Ben turned an eye toward Canada. He had proposed that the United Kingdom grant those northern lands to the colonies in 1760 in a pamphlet, *The Interest of Great Britain Considered with Regard to her Colonies and Acquisitions of Canada and Guadaloupe* and again after the French and Indian War in 1763.

Propositions were also made to the colonies' northern neighbor during the American Revolutionary War to join the cause of expelling the British from North America as well. Additionally, there were a number of incursions by armed Americans acting as freelance military volunteers acting on their own accord seeking to lay a claim for their mother country in Canada extending into the 1830s.

Franklin continued his duties as America's ambassador to France until 1785. He seriously considered spending his final days among the friends he had made over the past nine years. The desire to return back to Philadelphia and family proved stronger.

Thomas Jefferson was appointed as the next Minister Plenipotentiary to France in May 1785. When asked by French Foreign Minister Charles Gravier, Comte de Vergennes, if he was to replace the esteemed Franklin — Jefferson replied: "No one can replace him, Sir; I am only his successor."

★ FORMING A MORE PERFECT UNION ★

The authority governing the new American nation was the framework originally established in the Articles of Confederation and Perpetual Union. The Articles of Confederation was inspired in part by Benjamin Franklin's Albany Plan of Union of 1754. The Articles of Confederation were drafted in 1776 by the Second Continental Congress and ratified by the states in 1777. This Confederation brought America's United States together into a "firm league of friendship."

To mirror the transformation of the governing structure in 1781, the Congress likewise transformed into the Congress of the Confederation. It would remain identified as such until 1789. It was in February 1787 that the Congress agreed to call for a Constitutional Convention and thereby mend and amend the Articles of Confederation.

The Philadelphia Convention convened on May 25, 1787. It was presided over by George Washington and set to the task of devising means of perfecting their perpetual union. There were two sets of forces among the architects laying the foundations of a national government. Each of these forces had a different view on how much power to vest in a governing body.

George Washington (1732-1799), first president of the United States.

Illustration based on the 1796 portrait by Gilbert Stuart.

One faction preferred the current confederation of separate sovereign states. The states would join together for their mutual interests but maintain very individualized and specific states' rights in governing their own affairs. The opposing coalition sought to build a strong and centralized federal government. This central government would have the power to levy taxes, to create comprehensive and common laws of the land as well as to regulate interstate commerce. This became the clash of the Anti-Federalists and Federalists. It is a dispute of doctrines still at work in the American political discourse and ideologies to this day.

At the center of these proceedings was establishing the architecture of authority. The branches of the United States government are familiar today, but there was great controversy in the making of the blueprint. A number of plans went into the formation of America's federal foundations. They included a variety of configurations of legislative and executive powers. Benjamin Franklin, in fact, lobbied for a unicameral (single chamber) legislature. The members were to be elected solely in proportion to population. There would also be a twelve-member executive council to preside at the helm of the executive branch.

The Constitution of the United States of America has twenty-seven amendments. The first ten amendments are known as the Bill of Rights and were introduced by James Madison (1751–1836). The amendments were drafted in 1789 and ratified in 1791. The Eleventh Amendment was ratified in 1795. The most recent addition, the Twenty-Seventh Amendment, was ratified in 1992.

James Madison, who would later be elected the fourth president of the United States, is regarded as the father of the Constitution. His contribution, along with Alexander Hamilton (1755-1804) and John Jay (1745-1829), to *The Federalist Papers* made a compelling case for the framework and structure of the Constitution.

James Madison
Illustration based on the
1816 portrait by John Vanderlyn
(1775–1852)

Read the *US Constitution For Beginners* for an analysis of crucial elements of this binding set of principles in America's most critical legal document. Though hotly debated and constantly reinterpreted, the Constitution has survived wars, industrialization, expansion, and politicians. *US Constitution For Beginners* is written by Steve Bachmann and illustrated by Jorge Diaz.

US CONSTITUTION
FOR BEGINNERS
We the People

BY STEVE BACHMANN • ILLUSTRATIONS BY JORGE DIAZ
Courtesy of For Beginners

On June 28, 1787, Franklin introduced a motion designed to move his fellow delegates into a more collegial disposition. The Constitutional Convention brought together a collection of some of the greatest minds of the age, and thus there was an abundance of strong opinions. Each was confident in his own correctness.

Ben proposed that the Convention begin each day's session with a prayer as led by a clergyman. Franklin believed that this would prompt the members to put aside their own individual egos and recognize that there was a higher purpose that they were all working toward together. This initiative failed to gain support among the divisive body. In fact, Alexander Hamilton reportedly said that it wasn't necessary to make a bid for "foreign aid" by appealing to a higher power.

At the closing of the Convention, Benjamin Franklin gave remarks that were perhaps one of the most powerful statements of his long career in public service. He made an impassioned plea to bring an end to the quarrelsome climate and bridge the divisions among the delegates:

> I confess that there are several parts of this Constitution which I do not at present approve, but I am not sure I shall never approve them: For having lived long, I have experienced many instances of being obliged by better information, or fuller consideration, to change opinions even on important subjects, which I once thought right, but found to be otherwise. It is therefore that the older I grow, the more apt I am to doubt my own judgment, and to pay more respect to the judgment of others...

> In these sentiments, Sir, I agree to this Constitution with all its faults, if they are such; because I think a general Government necessary for us, and there is no form of Government but what may be a blessing to the people if well administered, and believe farther that this is likely to be well administered for a course of years, and can only end in Despotism, as other forms have done before it, when the people shall become so corrupted as to need despotic Government, being incapable of any other. I doubt too whether any other Convention we can obtain, may be able to make a better Constitution. For when you assemble a number of men to have the advantage of their joint wisdom, you inevitably assemble with those men, all their prejudices, their passions, their errors of opinion, their local interests, and their selfish views. From

such an assembly can a perfect production be expected? It therefore astonishes me, Sir, to find this system approaching so near to perfection as it does; and I think it will astonish our enemies, who are waiting with confidence to hear that our councils are confounded like those of the Builders of Babel; and that our States are on the point of separation, only to meet hereafter for the purpose of cutting one another's throats. Thus I consent, Sir, to this Constitution because I expect no better, and because I am not sure, that it is not the best...

On the whole, Sir, I can not help expressing a wish that every member of the Convention who may still have objections to it, would with me, on this occasion doubt a little of his own infallibility, and to make manifest our unanimity, put his name to this instrument.

During the many debates and deliberations, Franklin often found his gaze lingering on a carved design on the back of George Washington's chair. It was a scene that depicted the sun half-obscured by the horizon. Ben was endlessly speculating on whether the sun was rising or setting on the promise of the new American day — depending on the prevailing mood at the Convention.

All of the clamor and disputes that had been part of the fabric of the Convention when it began on May 25 had smoothed out when it came to an end nearly three months later. The Constitution of the United States of America was adopted by the Congress on September 17, 1787. Ben finally had his answer: The sun was rising.

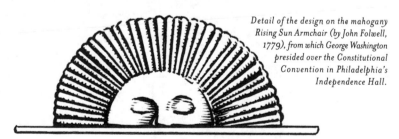

Detail of the design on the mahogany Rising Sun Armchair (by John Folwell, 1779), from which George Washington presided over the Constitutional Convention in Philadelphia's Independence Hall.

Reportedly, Benjamin Franklin was approached by a woman on the street soon after, who inquired, "What sort of government have you given us?" Franklin is said to have responded, "A republic, Madam, if you can keep it."

The Constitution of the United States (top) and the Bill of Rights (right) were ratified on June 21, 1788 and December 15, 1791, respectively. These documents established the framework of the American government.

★ FREEDOM FIGHTER ★

The Constitution of the United States of America was a new dawning in the manner in which a people — we, the people — might govern themselves. With any new day and bold beginning, there will be some shadows cast — a darkness that belies the brilliance of that first light.

In that time, some fundamental ideals were betrayed in the interest of practicality. Concessions and compromises were made to keep the slaveholding South joined with the free states of the North. The institution of slavery was left alone in order to preserve the Union. Slavery was not made part of the Constitution, but it was indirectly addressed and its advancement regulated.

This contamination of America's founding principles was left as a loose end and an open question. In time, it became a festering wound that the country would have to acknowledge and amend. The North believed that they had a provision to bring slavery to an end. The South believed they had firmly established the practice into the foundation of the new nation. This accommodation brought together a divided nation in a marriage of convenience, but would ultimately be drive it apart again by the American Civil War some seventy-four years later.

Benjamin Franklin's fight for liberty and the self-evident truth that all men were created equal didn't stop with those of his own complexion. Franklin had seen and heard the bitterness and arguments among the members of the Congress of the Confederation when addressing the issue of slavery when drafting the Constitution. He decided to address the issue head-on in the final chapter of his public life.

To be direct, Benjamin Franklin did profit from the slave economy in the past. In his days as a printer he would publish notices and advertisements for the trading of slaves and indentured labor. He also

Indentured labor was typically a period of service which was three to seven years. A European immigrant would enter an indenture contract with a land owner or business owner who would pay for their transatlantic journey to America — as well as provide food, lodging, and other staples — and in exchange the indentured servant would work for that individual for a specified period of time. These indentures were either entered into directly with the end user or contracted with a ship's captain (who would later sell the indenture agreement).

counted two African slaves, George and King, among his property during his days in the printing trade as well as at other times during his life.

Benjamin Franklin's views of liberty evolved. He became an ardent abolitionist in his later years and was named president of the Pennsylvania Society for Promoting the Abolition of Slavery in 1787. In February 1790, Franklin and the Pennsylvania Society for Promoting the Abolition of Slavery presented a petition to the Congress to put an end to this practice. It was received respectfully, but met with resistance by the Congress, which was weary of the debate. The petition was quietly ignored and ultimately tabled.

Courtesy of the Library of Congress

The anti-slavery petition that Franklin presented to the Congress.

Ben took his parting shot on the cause in the March 23, 1790 edition of *The Federal Gazette* with his clever "Address of Sidi Mehemet Ibrahim" ruse. (Read more about this incident in Part Three on pp. 61-62.) Franklin's final hoax was aimed at exposing the hypocrisy of arguments in favor of maintaining the institution of slavery.

Benjamin Franklin died less than four weeks later on April 17, 1790 at the age of eighty-four, fighting for freedom until the very end.

FOUNDER AND FRAMER:

A CHRONOLOGY

1768	Appointed colonial agent for Georgia
1769	Appointed colonial agent for New Jersey
1771	Appointed colonial agent for Massachusetts
1775	Chosen delegate to the Second Continental Congress
1776	Signs the Declaration of Independence
	Arrives in Paris to serve as a commissioner in diplomatic mission to France
1778	Signs the Treaties of Amity and Commerce
1783	Signs the Treaty of Paris
1787	Signs the Constitution of the United States of America
1789	Named president of the Society for Promoting the Abolition of Slavery
1790	Presents the Pennsylvania Society for Promoting the Abolition of Slavery petition to Congress

The Benjamin Franklin Memorial at the Franklin Institute in Philadelphia, Pennsylvania.

PART SEVEN

LIFE
and
LEGACY

Benjamin Franklin's story has meaning for all of us. It belongs to us. Franklin's journey from truant teen to timeless titan is a story of audacity... and dreaming, daring, and doing. The theme and narrative of this story would just happen to be Benjamin Franklin's greatest invention of all: the American Dream.

Benjamin Franklin is one of us. Franklin was solidly grounded in his middle-class status. He celebrated his humble beginnings and would proudly proclaim himself a printer and a leather apron man until the end of his days.

Despite all of his achievements and his associations with the high society of Philadelphia, London, and Paris, he had no aristocratic pretensions. In fact, Franklin would be famously antagonistic to the snobbery of those who owed their place in the social strata based on what family they had happened to be born into. Ben shunned the impractical and the showy in his possessions and in his person. Everything he needed came from within — from the incorruptible content of his character to the boundless brilliance of his mind.

Franklin moved forward in life on his own steam. His trajectory continues to be an inspiration to the generations of Americans who would follow in his footsteps or admire his path. It's been some 220 years since the end of his journey, but we're still talking about Benjamin Franklin. And there's still so much worth talking about.

★ FRANKLIN FINALE ★

Benjamin Franklin reportedly said as he was breathing his last that "a dying man can do nothing easily." He passed away on April 17, 1790 at the age of eighty-four with his dutiful grandsons and former international traveling companions, Temple and Benny, at his bedside. Also by his side during his last days were his daughter Sally and his surrogate daughter, Polly Hewson (daughter of former London landlady, Margaret Stevenson).

Franklin never claimed any religion as his own, although he was an adherent to Calvinism in his youth. Franklin's faith was more free-form as he was more of a deist and was unrestricted by doctrine and dogma. He did, however, recognize and show respect to virtually any organized religion by donating to any and all who asked. One could say that he hedged his bets by doing so, in the event that the afterlife reflected the views of any one faith more than the others. Members of the clergy for all Philadelphia faith communities were represented at Franklin's funeral procession of 20,000 mourners.

Benjamin Franklin, from the Laurence Hutton Collection of Life and Death Masks at Princeton University.

Within America's newly built halls of power, tributes to the memory of Franklin were (regrettably) restrained among many of his contemporaries. The French, however, held nothing back in their praise and admiration of Benjamin Franklin. Honoré-Gabriel Riqueti, comte de Mirabeau made a motion in the French National Assembly to memorialize France's favorite American:

Would it not become us, gentlemen, to join in this religious act, to bear a part in this homage, rendered, in the face of the world, both to the rights of man and to the philosopher who has most contributed to extend their sway over the whole earth? Antiquity would have raised altars to this mighty genius, who, to the advantage of mankind, compassing in his mind the heavens and the earth, was able to restrain alike thunderbolts and tyrants. Europe, enlightened and free, owes at least a token of remembrance and regret to one of the greatest men who have ever been engaged in the service of philosophy and liberty. I propose that it be decreed that the National Assembly, during three days shall wear mourning for Benjamin Franklin.

Franklin was interred next to Deborah at the Christ Church Burial Ground at Fifth and Arch Streets in Philadelphia. A simple six-foot slab would mark the burial place, adorned with only the unassuming "Benjamin and Deborah Franklin 1790" (much less flamboyant than the epitaph the twenty-two-year-old Franklin had drafted for himself — see Part Two, p. 25). The final resting place of Benjamin Franklin is, fittingly, within sight of Independence Hall and the National Constitution Center. The constant stream of visitors and tourists to the gravesite toss pennies on Franklin's marble marker for good luck.

★ THE FRANKLIN FAMILY ★

Benjamin Franklin was truly one of the great polymaths. He was a renaissance man without equal in the American pantheon. It's astonishing to even imagine there might be something at which he may not have excelled. However, no true portrait of an individual may be complete without the blemishes or those unpleasant moments that make us all human.

There was one area where Franklin's performance doesn't quite measure up to his other accomplishments, and that was the priority Ben placed on his own family. Benjamin Franklin may have put his incredible industry into numerous arenas and his seemingly immortal gift to the future of the American people. However, with all of the amazing achievements of Benjamin Franklin, he may have taken for granted what was right in front of him: his own flesh and blood.

It was in Franklin's last years, when the importance of family drew him back to America from abroad. It was Franklin's desire to spend his remaining days among his family and enjoy his grandchildren (as well as observe the infant republic start to learn how to gain its footing) and become reacquainted with his daughter.

There are no current descendants of Benjamin Franklin who can trace their ancestry directly back to Franklin himself.

★

*Benjamin Franklin
designed his own
family coat of arms.*

*Elements from Franklin's
(particularly the dolphin) as well
as from William Penn's coat of arms
were incorporated into the design of
the University of Pennsylvania crest.*

Benjamin Franklin's father, JOSIAH FRANKLIN (1657-1744), emigrated from England to the colony of Massachusetts with his wife and three children in 1684. The couple had four more children before Anne Franklin died in 1689.

Josiah soon took another wife, ABIAH FOLGER FRANKLIN, later that year in 1689. Josiah and Abiah Franklin had another ten children together that would further expand the Franklin family. Benjamin Franklin was the tenth son and the fifteenth of seventeen children fathered by Josiah Franklin.

Josiah's preference for his son was to be one of the clergy, a path in which young Ben Franklin seemed uninterested. He also did not show any interest in the many other vocations that the elder Franklin would introduce to his son. Josiah ultimately put the boy in service of his elder son James and into the printing business.

★

Benjamin Franklin's older brother, JAMES FRANKLIN (1697-1735), played a significant role in Ben's formative years as detailed in Franklin's *Autobiography*. James was Ben's master in their apprenticeship contract (and seems to have been a harsh one at that according to the younger Franklin's telling — see Part One, pp. 12-13). Despite Ben's views of his brother, James Franklin gave the young Benjamin Franklin valuable training and a good start in the printing trade.

James Franklin published *The New England Courant* from 1721 to 1726. It was in that paper that the young Ben Franklin's celebrated Silence Dogood hoaxes appeared (see Part Three, pp. 46-49). After relocating to Rhode Island, James published an almanac (occasionally under the name of "Poor Robin"), *Rhode-Island Almanack*, from 1727 to 1735. He would also publish the *Rhode Island Gazette* from 1732 to 1733.

When James died in 1735, Ben helped out his sister-in-law Ann by sending hundreds of copies of *Poor Richard's Almanac* as well as other publications so that she could sell them and earn an income. Ben and Deborah also took in James' son James to live with them from 1737 to 1748.

★

Benjamin Franklin caught the eye of his future wife, DEBORAH READ ROGERS FRANKLIN (1708-1774), as the seventeen-year-old Franklin walked the streets of Philadelphia for the first time in 1723. And she caught his eye. After a short-lived romance, the two later reconnected and began to share a life together in a common-law marriage in 1730 (see Part One, p. 21).

There is little doubt that Benjamin Franklin eventually outgrew his wife socially. He would travel in different circles than she. That may have created a rift, as Franklin's ambitions would carry him farther and farther from Philadelphia. Some biographers seem to have taken their own positions in their appraisals of Benjamin Franklin's wife of thirty-eight years. Some have called her "illiterate" and hinted that she was unworthy of someone like Franklin. Others have given a more sympathetic view of the long-suffering spouse separated by an ocean from her partner that she would tenderly call "Pappy."

Deborah Read Rogers Franklin
Illustration based on the 1758-59 portrait
by Benjamin Wilson (1721–1788).

In truth, the woman for whom he wrote the song "My Plain Country Joan" may have been less than the love of his life and more a sturdy partner. It's difficult to know the contents of a man's mind who may or may not have considered himself "married" in the conventional or legal sense.

Deborah had made numerous pleas in her letters to Ben for him to come home while he was in London from 1764 to 1775. He always seemed to have pressing matters of state that would further detain him. Ultimately, Franklin would still be far from home — for a period of ten years — when Deborah died at the age of sixty-six from a stroke.

★

The birth of WILLIAM FRANKLIN (1731-1813) is one of the biggest mysteries in the Benjamin Franklin story. Ben had begun living with Deborah Read in 1731 and within just months after they had begun their life together, Franklin presented her with a son he had fathered with another woman.

The identity of the mother of William Franklin has long been a topic of speculation and interest. But after almost three centuries since the birth of Franklin's first and only surviving son, scholars and history sleuths are still no closer to discovering the answer.

William Franklin
Illustration based on the 1790
portrait by Mather Brown
(1761-1831).

Ben and William shared a close relationship. William was ever-present at his father's side, and he was there with him on the day of the history-making kite experiment in 1752. Franklin was especially protective of William in light of Deborah's indifference (and at times hostility) toward the boy. Ben was vigilant against those who would make slights or call attention to William's illegitimate birth (particularly with the label of "bastard").

In time, perhaps through the direct or indirect influence of Benjamin Franklin, William was appointed as Royal Governor of New Jersey. The "natural bonds of affection" between Ben and William would become strained and were ultimately broken when the two chose different sides in the American Revolutionary War. Ben turned his back on his firstborn son out of wounded pride and an insistence that William give him the loyalty that he hadn't even given to his own father.

Upon William's arrest in 1776 as a Tory (that is, a British sympathizer), Ben refused to intervene on his son's behalf and request any sort of leniency or special treatment for the Royal Governor of New Jersey, who was now under arrest by the American Continental Army. William was ultimately released in 1778 and would leave America in 1782 to spend the rest of his days in England.

★

FRANCIS FOLGER FRANKLIN (1732-1736) or Franky as his father called him, was clearly one of the great delights of Ben's life. Franky was born to Benjamin Franklin and Deborah Read in 1732. The boy didn't come with the same emotional baggage that had accompanied young William and was surely a more welcome arrival as he was Deborah's own.

Tragically, the boy became infected with smallpox and died at the age of four. He was just recovering from the flux (now known as dysentery), and Ben was waiting for him to regain his strength before getting Franky inoculated to protect against smallpox.

Francis Folger Franklin

During those days, there was a heated debate over the practice of inoculations. Vaccinations for smallpox were a relatively recent development in the effort to combat this deadly menace of colonial life. The practice, however, was quite controversial based on the fears of contracting the disease rather than keeping someone safe from it. As Ben championed the cause of vaccination, he made sure to publish a regretful note in *The Pennsylvania Gazette* that his son had died of smallpox because he hadn't been inoculated and not because he had been.

★

SARAH FRANKLIN BACHE (1743-1808) was the second child born to Benjamin Franklin and Deborah Read Franklin. She was thirteen years old when Ben left for London in 1757 to take up his first five-year mission as agent for Pennsylvania.

Sarah, or "Sally" as she was called in the Franklin household, married Richard Bache in 1767 and would have eight children (including the firebrand Benjamin Franklin Bache). In her thirties, revolutionary zeal had overtaken her and she worked ceaselessly for the cause of American liberty. Ben left Sarah much of his estate upon his death. He left none to William, the son he considered a traitor to the American cause.

Sarah Franklin Bache
Illustration based on the 1793 portrait
by John Hoppner (1758-1810).

★

WILLIAM TEMPLE FRANKLIN (1760-1823), son of William Franklin, was born in London to a mother that has never been identified. He was the second generation of illegitimate sons (which would be a tradition that William Temple would continue).

William Temple, or "Temple" as he was often called, accompanied his grandfather on his diplomatic mission to Paris in 1776. Temple served as Secretary to the American delegation during the negotiations of the Treaty of Paris. Benjamin Franklin had requested new appointments for his grandson, but the Second Continental Congress refused the request (as a result of the factionalism and petty rivalries that were forming in the Congress).

William Temple Franklin had inherited his grandfather's papers and was his literary executor (that is, the person responsible for publishing his papers after Franklin's death). The official *Autobiography of Benjamin Franklin*, edited by William Temple Franklin, was published in 1818. This was some twenty-seven years after the incomplete French translation, *Mémoires de la vie privée de Benjamin Franklin*, was published in Paris in 1791.

★

BENJAMIN FRANKLIN BACHE (1769-1798), named for his famous grandfather, was the son of Sarah Franklin Bache and Richard Bache. Young Benny, along with his cousin William Temple Franklin, was part of Benjamin Franklin's staff on the French diplomatic mission to Paris.

Benny inherited Benjamin Franklin's printing presses and equipment and followed

Masthead of THE AURORA AND GENERAL ADVERTISER.

in the footsteps of his noteworthy namesake. He published *The Aurora*, a newspaper that gained the reputation of being passionately anti-Federalist. The newspaper brought the anger of the Adams Administration on him under the short-lived Sedition Act. (The Sedition Act made it illegal to publish "false, scandalous, and malicious writing" about the government — it also violated the First Amendment's protection of free speech).

Benjamin Franklin Bache's young and bright light was extinguished at the age of twenty-nine when he died from yellow fever.

★ NAMING RITES ★

There is no greater claim to fame than those things that have one's name attached to them. Those structures, objects, and persons remain as permanent markers of one's accomplishments. Whether a towering building or distinguished institution, town or street, county or company, or even a president of the United States — those things that endure ensure the continuing memory and living legacy of those who have gone before.

Benjamin Franklin has been honored just so across the nation. Following are only a few examples that memorialize Benjamin Franklin...

★

FRANKLINIA ALATAMAHA is a small deciduous tree discovered by botanists John and William Bartram in 1765 and named in honor of Ben Franklin.

★

There have been six U.S. Naval vessels named for Benjamin Franklin including:

USS *Bonhomme Richard*: A former merchant ship, the vessel was acquired by King Louis XVI in 1779 and then put under the command of John Paul Jones. The ship was actually named in tribute to Franklin's "Poor Richard" persona from his famous almanac (and there would be three more ships so named). The *Bonhomme Richard* was ultimately lost in battle just eight months after going into service.

USS *Franklin*: A six-gun schooner was requisitioned and commissioned in 1775 during the Revolutionary War for the Continental Navy and ultimately returned to her original owner in 1776.

John Paul Jones (1747- 1792), the legendary Scottish sailor famously quipped "I have not yet begun to fight," during the epic battle with the HMS SERAPIS that sank the BONHOMME RICHARD.

Illustration based on the 1890 portrait by George Bagby Matthews (1857-1943).

USS *Franklin* II: An eight-gun brig commissioned in 1795. This second USS *Franklin* was captured by Barbary pirates during the Tripolitan Wars in 1802. The ship was purchased back from the Barbary States by a commercial agent in 1805.

USS *Franklin* III: A seventy-four-gun vessel built in 1815, it served in the Mediterranean and Pacific before being dispatched to Boston in 1843. The ship was ultimately demolished in 1852.

USS *Franklin* IV: The fourth U.S. Naval vessel to carry the name of Franklin was a thirty-nine-gun frigate launched in 1864 and commissioned in 1867. The ship was deployed to the North Atlantic before returning to Norfolk in 1877 before being decommissioned in 1915.

USS *Franklin* V (CV-13): An Essex class aircraft carrier commissioned in 1944 and removed from the Naval Registration in 1964.

★

For a brief period from 1784 to 1790, there was a STATE OF FRANKLIN (originally Frankland for the "Land of the Free"). Eight counties seceded from western North Carolina and had petitioned the Continental Congress to join the Union as a sovereign state. The State of Franklin's efforts to join the Union failed to gain the two-thirds majority vote in the Continental Congress as required by the Articles of Confederation. The territory ultimately joined with Tennessee in 1790.

The Tripolitan War (or the First Barbary War) proved to be the first major foreign challenge to the presidency of Thomas Jefferson. From 1801 to 1805, American merchant and naval ships were continually preyed on by pirates along the Barbary Coast of northwestern Africa. The pirates would demand ransoms for the return of vessels and crew until the Jefferson Administration determined that it was necessary to put an end to the ongoing threat and launched a campaign of raids and blockades of the ports of the aggressors. The American victory has been immortalized in the "Marines' Hymn" by the reference "to the shores of Tripoli."

★

Benjamin Franklin was also associated with the founding of another academy of higher learning in 1787. Founded by ministers from the Reformed Church and Lutheran Church in Lancaster, Pennsylvania, this institution had a mission "to preserve our present republican system of government" and "to promote those improvements in the arts and sciences which alone render nations respectable, great and happy."

FRANKLIN COLLEGE was named for Ben Franklin in recognition of a generous contribution of £200. The College later merged with Marshall College (named for Supreme Court Chief Justice John Marshall) in 1853, becoming Franklin and Marshall College.

★

FRANKLIN SQUARE, originally named Northeast Square, was rechristened in honor of Benjamin Franklin in 1825. The square was intended to be one of Philadelphia's five public squares as set aside in William Penn's city plan. Today, the Square (managed by Historic Philadelphia, Inc.) is home to such attractions as the Liberty Carousel, Philly Mini Golf, the Franklin Square Fountain, and a playground.

★

Now known as THE FRANKLIN INSTITUTE, The Franklin Institute of the State of Pennsylvania for the Promotion of the Mechanic Arts was founded in February 1824 to showcase the ingenious inventions of Benjamin Franklin. The Institute would become a hands-on science museum and would thereafter be identified as The Franklin Institute Science Museum in January 1934.

Today, The Franklin Institute is Philadelphia's preeminent science museum and is located just off of the Benjamin Franklin Parkway. The Institute is home to celebrated exhibits such as the Giant Heart, the Train Factory, and Space Command as well as the famed Fels Planetarium.

THE GIANT HEART first opened in 1954 and is over 5,000 square feet.

★

An impact crater on the Moon is also named after Benjamin Franklin. The FRANKLIN CRATER is located on the northeast area of the Moon's visible surface with a lunar latitude of 38.8°N and longitude of 47.7°E. The crater has a diameter of 56 km and depth of 3.82 km.

German astronomers Johann Heinrich von Mädler and Wilhelm Beer identified and named the Franklin crater in their exhaustive cartography of the Moon in their "Mappa Selenographica" in 1836 as well as in their 1837 book, Der Mond (The Moon).

Franklin Crater, the Moon

★

The fourteenth president of the United States, FRANKLIN PIERCE, was named after Benjamin Franklin and served as chief executive from 1853-1857. Pierce served at a difficult time in American history, with the Civil War looming on the near horizon. His presidency proved to be unsuccessful and he was replaced at the head of the Democratic ticket by James Buchanan in the 1856 presidential election. Franklin Pierce University of Pierce's native New Hampshire was named in his honor.

Franklin Pierce (1804-1869)
Illustration based on the 1853 portrait
by George Peter Alexander Healy
(1818–1894).

★

The oldest football stadium still in operation in America is named for Benjamin Franklin at the very university that he helped found. The University of Pennsylvania built FRANKLIN FIELD in 1895 and it is where football, lacrosse, field hockey, and track-and-field events still occur to this day. Franklin Field also gave home field advantage to the Philadelphia Eagles from 1958 to 1970.

★

Benjamin Franklin was famously a printer first and foremost. His expertise in the art of typography is evident in his beautifully crafted published pieces and periodicals. FRANKLIN GOTHIC was a font that was designed by Morris Fuller Benton in 1902 as a tribute to Benjamin Franklin and his contribution to the profession of printing and graphic design.

Franklin Gothic is a typeface that is ideal for use in headlines and other display treatments. A number of fonts have been created in honor of Benjamin Franklin over the years as well.

Franklin Gothic

abcdefghijklmnopqrstuvwxyz[äöüßåøæœç]
ABCDEFGHIJKLMNOPQRSTUVWXYZ
1234567890(.,;:?!$¢€£¥&-*){ÄÖÜÅØÆŒÇ}

► **Regular**
The quick brown fox jumps over a Dog. Zwei Boxkämpfer jagen Eva durch Sylt portez ce vieux Whiskey blond qui fume une pipe aber

► **Extra Condensed**
The quick brown fox jumps over a Dog. Zwei Boxkämpfer jagen Eva durch Sylt portez ce vieux Whiskey blond qui fume une pipe aber echt über die Mauer gesprungen und auch smørebrød en

► **Condensed**
The quick brown fox jumps over a Dog. Zwei Boxkämpfer jagen Eva durch Sylt portez ce vieux Whiskey blond qui fume une pipe aber echt über die Mauer ge-

Courtesy of FSI FontShop International

★

The BENJAMIN FRANKLIN NATIONAL MEMORIAL is located in the rotunda at The Franklin Institute in Philadelphia. A twenty-foot tall, thirty-ton marble statue of a seated Franklin on a ninety-two-ton marble pedestal sculpted by James Earle Fraser between 1906 to 1911. The statue is central to the Pantheon-inspired memorial hall designed by architect John T. Windrim. The memorial was dedicated in 1938 and is administered by The Franklin Institute and the National Park Service.

★

The BENJAMIN FRANKLIN INSTITUTE OF TECHNOLOGY was founded in 1908 in Boston with money from twin funds that were donated to Philadelphia and Boston. Ben had directed that £1000 be left to each city in separate trusts for the purposes of making loans to tradesmen in establishing their own business. After 200 years, the funds were dispersed to benefit trade schools and fund scholarships.

★

One of Philadelphia's most distinctive boulevards is the BENJAMIN FRANKLIN PARKWAY. It stretches a tree-and-museum-lined mile from Philadelphia City Hall to Eakins Oval (in front of the Philadelphia Museum of Art). The Parkway — designed by French architect and urban planner Jacques Gréber in 1916 — was built to be a "a slice of Paris in Philadelphia" and emulate the Champs-Élysées. Construction was completed in 1935 on the parkway, which has set the stage for many parades and events in Philadelphia.

★

The BENJAMIN FRANKLIN BRIDGE, formerly known as the Delaware River Bridge until 1956, spans the Delaware River and connects Philadelphia to Camden, New Jersey. The bridge, constructed in 1926, was the longest suspension bridge in the world until 1929 with a total length of 9,753 feet and its longest span being 1,750 feet.

A 101-foot-tall, 60-ton sculpture of a kite and lightning bolt stands at the Philadelphia-facing end of the bridge as a memorial to Benjamin Franklin. "Bolt of Lightning" by Isamu Noguchi was actually designed and proposed in 1933, but installation would have to wait until 1984, when contemporary culture caught up with the forward-thinking artist.

BOLT OF LIGHTNING, 1984
Isamu Noguchi

★

FRANKLIN DELANO ROOSEVELT, the thirty-second president of the United States, was another prominent American named after Benjamin Franklin. Commonly referred to as "FDR," the Democratic governor of New York defeated incumbent Republican president Herbert Hoover in the 1932 presidential election. America was faced with some grave challenges during the unprecedented four-term presidency of Roosevelt, including the Great Depression and World War II. FDR died in office of a stroke on April 12, 1945. He was succeeded by his vice president, Harry Truman (1884-1972).

★

FRANKLIN TEMPLETON INVESTMENTS is an international investment and wealth management firm headquartered in San Mateo, California. The company, which got its start in 1947, specializes in mutual funds and retirement accounts.

★

The FRANKLIN MINT, founded in 1964 and located in Exton, Pennsylvania, has become an American household name with its collectibles, including coins, jewelry, models, dolls, and other keepsakes.

The Franklin Mint also produced THE FRANKLIN LIBRARY of fine bound editions of great book collections that it offered on a subscription basis from 1973 to 2000.

Read *FDR and the New Deal For Beginners* and learn more about the history of the precedent-making administration of Franklin Delano Roosevelt (1882-1945) through the bitter economic depression and the New Deal's expansive programs empowering artists and working people and how it became the grandest social experiment in the history of American democracy. For the first time, the lives of the president, the first lady, and the ordinary people of the time are seen through an inventive comic narrative accompanying historic illustrations and a sympathetic, but not uncritical text. *FDR and the New Deal For Beginners* is written by Paul Buhle with comics by Sabrina Jones.

Courtesy of For Beginners

★

FRANKLIN COURT is the site of Benjamin Franklin's Philadelphia home and offices on 314–322 Market Street. Administered by the National Park Service, Franklin Court was dedicated in 1976 as part of the Park Service's bicentennial celebration.

At the heart of Franklin Court stands the Ghost Structure House by architect Robert Venturi. Widely referred to as the "Ghost House," the structure traces an outline of where Benjamin Franklin's house once stood in three-dimensional space. (The house was pulled down in 1812 by Franklin's misguided grandchildren to parcel off the land for profitable row homes.)

An underground museum as well as a post office, postal museum, printing office, and

GHOST HOUSE, 1976
Robert Venturi

the restored space of *The Aurora and General Advertiser* (the newspaper published by Ben's grandson, Benjamin Franklin Bache) are also maintained on the site.

★

The BEN FRANKLIN TECHNOLOGY PARTNERS is a Pennsylvania technology-based economic development program. It was founded in 1983 for the purpose of accelerating and stimulating technological advancement and commercialization. The program is an initiative of the Pennsylvania Department of Community and Economic Development and is funded by the Ben Franklin Technology Development Authority.

★

FRANKLIN MILLS MALL, opened in 1989, is a Greater Philadelphia shopping mall known for discount shopping and great brands with more than 200 retail stores, restaurants, and movie theater.

World-renowned graphic designer Milton Glaser designed the identity and signage system with the well-known kite and lightning motif for this popular Philadelphia-area shopping destination.

★

The BENJAMIN FRANKLIN TERCENTENARY is a private/non-profit partnership. It took the lead in overseeing the official 300th anniversary of the birth of Benjamin Franklin. The Tercentenary, noted for its "Benjamin Franklin: In Search of a Better World" traveling exhibition, was established in 2000 by a coalition including the American Philosophical Society, the Franklin Institute, the Library Company of Philadelphia, the Philadelphia Museum of Art, and the University of Pennsylvania.

★

The BENJAMIN FRANKLIN HOUSE is a museum dedicated to Benjamin Franklin in the former home of Margaret Stevenson. Franklin resided there at Number 7 Craven Street (now Number 36 Craven Street) in London during his 1757-1762 and 1764-1775 periods of service as a colonial agent. The Benjamin Franklin House opened to the public on January 17, 2006, on what would have been Ben's 300th birthday.

LIFE AND LEGACY:

A CHRONOLOGY

1657	Birth of Josiah Franklin (died 1745)
1667	Birth of Abiah Folger Franklin (died 1752)
1697	Birth of James Franklin (died 1735)
1706	Birth of Benjamin Franklin (died 1790)
1708	Birth of Deborah Read Rogers Franklin (died 1774)
1731	Birth of William Franklin (died 1813)
1732	Birth of Francis Folger Franklin (died 1736)
1743	Birth of Sarah Franklin Bache (died 1808)
1760	Birth of William Temple Franklin (died 1823)
1765	Franklinia Alatamaha discovered
1769	Birth of Benjamin Franklin Bache (died 1798)
1775	USS *Franklin* christened (decommissioned 1776)
1779	USS *Bonhomme Richard* christened (sunk 1779)
1784	State of Franklin founded (dissolved 1790)
1787	Franklin College founded (later named Franklin and Marshall)
1795	USS *Franklin II* christened (decommissioned 1807)
1804	Birth of Franklin Pierce (died 1869)
1815	USS *Franklin III* built (decommissioned 1852)
1824	The Franklin Institute founded
1825	Franklin Square dedicated
1836	Franklin Crater discovered
1867	USS *Franklin IV* built (decommissioned 1915)
1882	Birth of Franklin Delano Roosevelt (died 1945)
1895	Franklin Field constructed
1902	Franklin Gothic font created
1908	Benjamin Franklin Institute of Technology founded
1926	Benjamin Franklin Bridge constructed
1935	Benjamin Franklin Parkway construction completed
1938	Benjamin Franklin National Memorial dedicated
1947	Franklin Templeton Investments founded
1964	Franklin Mint founded
1976	Franklin Court dedicated
1983	Ben Franklin Technology Partners founded
1984	Bolt of Lightning sculpture erected
1989	Franklin Mills Mall opened
2000	Benjamin Franklin Tercentenary Commission established
2006	Benjamin Franklin House opened

BIBLIOGRAPHY

Benjamin Franklin House. "About the House." BenjaminFranklinHouse.org.
www.benjaminfranklinhouse.org/site/sections/about_house/

The Benjamin Franklin Tercentenary. "Benjamin Franklin: In Search of
a Better World." BenFranklin300.org. www.benfranklin300.org

Blumberg, Jess. "A Brief History of the Salem Witch Trials." Smithsonian.com.
www.smithsonianmag.com/history-archaeology/brief-salem.html

Brands, H.W. *Benjamin Franklin: The Original American*.
New York, NY: Barnes & Noble, 2004.

Brands, H.W. *The First American: The Life and Times of Benjamin Franklin*.
New York, NY: Anchor Books, 2002.

Clemens, Samuel L. *The Writings of Mark Twain*.
New York, NY: Harper & Brothers Publishers, 1917.

Cohen, I. Bernard. *Benjamin Franklin's Science*.
Cambridge: Harvard University Press, 1996.

Dray, Philip. *Stealing God's Thunder: Benjamin Franklin's Lightning Rod
and the Invention of America*. New York, NY: Random House, 2005.

Drinker Bowen, Catherine. *The Most Dangerous Man in America: Scenes from the
Life of Benjamin Franklin*. New York, NY: Little Brown & Co, 1986.

Ellis, Joseph J. *American Creation*. New York, NY: Alfred A. Knopf, 2007.

Ellis, Joseph J. *Founding Brothers*. New York, NY: Alfred A. Knopf, 2000.

Finger, Stanley. *Doctor Franklin's Medicine*.
Philadelphia, PA: University of Pennsylvania Press, 2006.

Fleming, Candace. *Ben Franklin's Almanac*.
New York, NY: Athenum Books For Young Readers, 2003.

Fleming, Thomas. *Ben Franklin: Inventing America*.
New York, NY: Sterling Point Books, 2007.

Fortune, Brandon Brame and Warner, Deborah J. *Franklin & His Friends*.
Philadelphia, PA: University of Pennsylvania Press, 1999.

Franklin, Benjamin. *The Autobiography of Benjamin Franklin*.
Philadelphia, PA: University of Pennsylvania Press, 2005.

Franklin, Benjamin. *Benjamin Franklin: Diplomat*.
Prince Frederick, MD: Recorded Books, 1999.

Franklin, Benjamin. "The Writings of Benjamin Franklin." HistoryCarper.com.
www.historycarper.com/category/essays/benjamin-franklin/

The Franklin Institute Science Museum. "Benjamin Franklin: Glimpses of the Man." FranklinInstitute.org. sln.fi.edu/franklin/

Goodman, Nathan G. *The Ingenious Dr. Franklin.* Philadelphia, PA: University of Pennsylvania Press, 1974.

Green, James N. and Stallybrass, Peter. "Benjamin Franklin: Writer and Printer." LibraryCompany.org. www.librarycompany.org/BFWriter/

Independence Hall Association. "The Electric Ben Franklin." UShistory.org. www.ushistory.org/franklin/

Isaacson, Walter. *Benjamin Franklin: An American Life.* New York, NY: Simon & Schuster, 2003.

Lemay, J.A. Leo. *The Life of Benjamin Volume 1.* Philadelphia, PA: University of Pennsylvania Press, 2006.

Lemay, J.A. Leo. *The Life of Benjamin Volume 2.* Philadelphia, PA: University of Pennsylvania Press, 2006.

The Library of Congress American Treasures Exhibition. "Benjamin Franklin... In His Own Words." LOC.gov. www.loc.gov/exhibits/treasures/franklin-printer.html

McCullough, David. *1776.* New York, NY: Simon & Schuster, 2005.

Schiff, Stacy. *A Great Improvisation: Franklin, France, and the Birth of America.* New York, NY: Henry Holt and Company, 2006.

Standage, Tom. "Monster in a Box" Wired.com. www.wired.com/wired/archive/10.03/turk_pr.html

Twilley, Nicola. "Six New Letters for a Reformed Alphabet." BenFranklin300.org. www.benfranklin300.org/_etc_pdf/Six_New_Letters_Nicola_Twilly.pdf

Twin Cities Public Television. "Benjamin Franklin: An Extraordinary Life. An Electric Mind." PBS.org. www.pbs.org/benfranklin/

University of Pennsylvania: Penn Medicine. "In the Beginning: The Story of the Creation of the Nation's First Hospital." PennMedicine.org. www.uphs.upenn.edu/paharc/features/creation.html

Wayne, Fredd. *Benjamin Franklin, Citizen.* Auburn, CA: Audio Partners, 1995.

Weems, M.L. *The Life of Benjamin Franklin.* Philadelphia, PA: Uriah Hunt & Son, 1854.

Wood, Gordon S. *The Americanization of Benjamin Franklin.* New York, NY: Penguin Books, 2005.

ACKNOWLEDGMENTS

I'm thankful to many who have accompanied me on this journey in the making of *Ben Franklin For Beginners*. Your support and assistance means more to me than I can say.

Thank you to the For Beginners team who've made this possible: Dawn Reshen Doty, Publisher; Merrilee Warholak, Editorial Director/ Managing Editor; Susan Poitras, Media Director; and Jessica Haberman, Editor. Thank you also to editor Bill Finan for giving *Ben Franklin For Beginners* a vigorous and thorough edit.

I'm grateful to the love, patience, and support of my family including my lovely wife Candice and our son Philip; my parents: Larry and Nancy Ogline; my sister and family: Jenna and Greg Deck, and my favorite nephew and niece Connor and Abby Hartman; my father and mother-in-law: Rick and Marlene DeBella; and my brother-in-law Rich DeBella.

I additionally want to thank my writer friends for your camaraderie and encouragement: Kimberly Nagy, Joy Stocke, Angie Brenner, Jonathan Maberry, John Koloski, and Marina Gottlieb Sarles.

These are the people that helped — the ones that answered questions and offered advice. Thank you:

Harold Cramer
mapsofpa.com

Marlene DeBella, Customer
Service Representative
University of Pennsylvania Press

Lynne Farrington, Curator
of Printed Books
Rare Book and Manuscript Library,
University of Pennsylvania

Bill Finan, Editor
University of Pennsylvania Press

Judy Hansen
Hansen Literary Agency

Nicole Joniec, Print Department
Assistant & Digital Collections Manager
Library Company of Philadelphia

Dana M. Lamparello, Digital
Collections Archivist
The Historical Society of Pennsylvania

Michael Pieracci
FontShop International

Diane Sharp, Director, Marketing
& Associate Director, Admissions
The Wharton School,
University of Pennsylvania

Stephen Sinon, Head of Information
Services and Archives
The LuEsther T. Mertz Library,
The New York Botanical Garden

Janice Stillman, Editor
Yankee Publishing Inc.

Page Talbott Ph.D., Principal
Remer & Talbott

Dee Venuto, Media Center Coordinator
Rancocas Valley Regional High School

Chuck Wood, Affiliate Scientist
Planetary Science Institute

Tim E. Ogline, a passionate student of American history with a particular interest in the American Revolution, is a Greater Philadelphia based illustrator and graphic designer. Ogline is an alumnus of Temple University's Tyler School of Art and has previously taught there. He is also currently an adjunct instructor at Moore College of Art & Design.

Ogline's illustrations have appeared in *The Wall Street Journal*, *The Philadelphia Inquirer*, the *Utne Reader*, *The American Spectator*, *Outdoor Life*, *Institutional Investor*, *Philadelphia Style*, *Loyola Lawyer*, *How Magazine*, the *Wild River Review*, and *The Florida Review* among others.

Tim Ogline's design practice, Ogline Design, serves a diverse client base; but has specialized in political and institutional sectors. Clients served include Historic Philadelphia, the Crossroads of the American Revolution Association, Pennsylvania Governor Ed Rendell, The White House, Lois Murphy for Congress, University of Pennsylvania Graduate School of Education, the Wharton School of the University of Pennsylvania, the National Governors Association, TargetX, the American Association for the Advancement of Science, Group Inc, Wild River Books, and many more with creative solutions that have ranged from identity design to publication design to website development.

THE FOR BEGINNERS® SERIES

AFRICAN HISTORY FOR BEGINNERS: ISBN 978-1-934389-18-8
ANARCHISM FOR BEGINNERS: ISBN 978-1-934389-32-4
ARABS & ISRAEL FOR BEGINNERS: ISBN 978-1-934389-16-4
ART THEORY FOR BEGINNERS: ISBN 978-1-934389-47-8
ASTRONOMY FOR BEGINNERS: ISBN 978-1-934389-25-6
AYN RAND FOR BEGINNERS: ISBN 978-1-934389-37-9
BARACK OBAMA FOR BEGINNERS, AN ESSENTIAL GUIDE: ISBN 978-1-934389-44-7
BLACK HISTORY FOR BEGINNERS: ISBN 978-1-934389-19-5
THE BLACK HOLOCAUST FOR BEGINNERS: ISBN 978-1-934389-03-4
BLACK WOMEN FOR BEGINNERS: ISBN 978-1-934389-20-1
CHOMSKY FOR BEGINNERS: ISBN 978-1-934389-17-1
DADA & SURREALISM FOR BEGINNERS: ISBN 978-1-934389-00-3
DANTE FOR BEGINNERS: ISBN 978-1-934389-67-6
DECONSTRUCTION FOR BEGINNERS: ISBN 978-1-934389-26-3
DEMOCRACY FOR BEGINNERS: ISBN 978-1-934389-36-2
DERRIDA FOR BEGINNERS: ISBN 978-1-934389-11-9
EASTERN PHILOSOPHY FOR BEGINNERS: ISBN 978-1-934389-07-2
EXISTENTIALISM FOR BEGINNERS: ISBN 978-1-934389-21-8
FDR AND THE NEW DEAL FOR BEGINNERS: ISBN 978-1-934389-50-8
FOUCAULT FOR BEGINNERS: ISBN 978-1-934389-12-6
GENDER & SEXUALITY FOR BEGINNERS: ISBN 978-1-934389-69-0
GLOBAL WARMING FOR BEGINNERS: ISBN 978-1-934389-27-0
GREEK MYTHOLOGY FOR BEGINNERS   ISBN 978-1-934389-83-6
HEIDEGGER FOR BEGINNERS: ISBN 978-1-934389-13-3
ISLAM FOR BEGINNERS: ISBN 978-1-934389-01-0
JANE AUSTEN FOR BEGINNERS: ISBN 978-1-934389-61-4
JUNG FOR BEGINNERS: ISBN 978-1-934389-76-8
KIERKEGAARD FOR BEGINNERS: ISBN 978-1-934389-14-0
LACAN FOR BEGINNERS: ISBN 978-1-934389-39-3
LINGUISTICS FOR BEGINNERS: ISBN 978-1-934389-28-7
MALCOLM X FOR BEGINNERS: ISBN 978-1-934389-04-1
MARX'S *DAS KAPITAL* FOR BEGINNERS: ISBN 978-1-934389-59-1
MCLUHAN FOR BEGINNERS: ISBN 978-1-934389-75-1
NIETZSCHE FOR BEGINNERS: ISBN 978-1-934389-05-8
PHILOSOPHY FOR BEGINNERS: ISBN 978-1-934389-02-7
PLATO FOR BEGINNERS: ISBN 978-1-934389-08-9
POETRY FOR BEGINNERS: ISBN 978-1-934389-46-1
POSTMODERNISM FOR BEGINNERS: ISBN 978-1-934389-09-6
RELATIVITY & QUANTUM PHYSICS FOR BEGINNERS: ISBN 978-1-934389-42-3
SARTRE FOR BEGINNERS: ISBN 978-1-934389-15-7
SHAKESPEARE FOR BEGINNERS: ISBN 978-1-934389-29-4
STRUCTURALISM & POSTSTRUCTURALISM FOR BEGINNERS: ISBN 978-1-934389-10-2
WOMEN'S HISTORY FOR BEGINNERS: ISBN 978-1-934389-60-7
UNIONS FOR BEGINNERS: ISBN 978-1-934389-77-5
U.S. CONSTITUTION FOR BEGINNERS: ISBN 978-1-934389-62-1
ZEN FOR BEGINNERS: ISBN 978-1-934389-06-5
ZINN FOR BEGINNERS: ISBN 978-1-934389-40-9

WWW.FORBEGINNERSBOOKS.COM